MARK YACONELLI

DOWNTIME
HELPING TEENAGERS PRAY

ZONDERVAN®

ZONDERVAN.com/
AUTHORTRACKER
follow your favorite authors

youth
specialties

**youth
specialties**

Downtime: Helping Teenagers Pray
Copyright 2008 by Mark Yaconelli

Youth Specialties resources, 300 S. Pierce St., El Cajon, CA 92020 are published by Zondervan, 5300 Patterson Ave. SE, Grand Rapids, MI 49530.

ISBN 978-0-310-28362-1

Web site addresses listed in this book were current at the time of publication. Please contact Youth Specialties via email (YS@YouthSpecialties.com) to report URLs that are no longer operational and replacement URLs if available.

Cover design by SharpSeven Design
Interior design by Mark Novelli, IMAGO MEDIA

Printed in the United States of America

09 10 11 12 • 20 19 18 17 16 15 14 13 12 11 10 9 8 7 6 5 4 3 2

DEDICATION

For my grandfather,

Earnest "Boppa" Yaconelli,

whose daily prayers have been the invisible angel on which much

of my life rests.

Teach us to pray.

—LUKE 11:1

When the church is no longer teaching the people how to pray, we could almost say it will have lost its reason for existence. Prayer is the ultimate empowerment of the people of God, and may be why we clerics prefer laws and guilt, though they often disempower us and make us live in insufficiency and doubt. Prayer, however, gives us a sense of abundance and connectedness.

—RICHARD ROHR

CONTENTS

LIST OF PRAYERS AND EXERCISES

ACKNOWLEDGMENTS

Once again my thanks to Chris Coble and the Lilly Endowment for providing the resources necessary to research and write this book. Thanks to Doug Davidson for shepherding this book into its final form. Thanks also to Jay Howver at Youth Specialties for his friendship and support. As always, my heart's gratitude and admiration goes to my wife, Jill, for her listening ear and thoughtful suggestions on the development of the manuscript.

INTRODUCTION
Slowing to the Speed of God

O God, You are my shepherd,

I shall not want;

You bring me to green pastures for rest

and lead me beside still waters

renewing my spirit;

You restore my soul.

You lead me in the path of goodness

to follow Love's way.

PSALM 23
NAN C. MERRILL, P*SALMS FOR PRAYING:
AN INVITATION TO WHOLENESS*[1]

Downtime is a book about tending the life of prayer within young people. It is a response to the yearning for prayer that lives within adolescents, and all of us who seek to follow Jesus. In my experience, young people crave the peace of Christ that waits beneath the frantic hamster wheel of modern soci-

[1] Continuum Publishing, 2007.

ety. They are longing—and often feel they need to be given permission—to set aside the many agendas, expectations, and amusements in which they find themselves entangled in order to stop and open themselves into God.

Just as young people need relationships, they need prayer. Young people are ripe for prayer because the core human struggles are so apparent in adolescence. Teenagers stand at the threshold of adult desires, with hearts that are soft and awake. Questions of identity and feelings of longing and suffering are breaking open in young people for the first time. They cry more often. They fall in love easily. They crave and seek friendships. They're inclined toward the ecstatic. We teach young people to pray so they'll know they're not alone; so they might find the source and endpoint of their restless desires; so they might find comfort and healing within an increasingly heartless and destructive world. To invite youth into prayer is to invite them to discover God within the heart of human experience.

For 10 years I regularly interviewed young people about their spiritual lives. I was fascinated by the way they often described their deepest encounters with God. For many, these experiences of God were moments of rest, solitude, silence, reflection, and contemplative wonder. They were experiences of "downtime." For young people, these encounters with God often took place as they lay on their beds at night pondering their life in God, or in moments in nature beholding sky, birds, and branches. Some spoke of solitary experiences of grief or loneliness when they were greeted by God's comfort or companionship. Others referred to worship experiences that seemed to exist in another time—embracing or holding the yearning of the world. Some young people talked about moments of love or service in which they found themselves carrying the suffering and beauty of life around them.

My hope is that this book will encourage a different pace within youth ministry, churches, and families—that it will inspire adults working with youth to be radical not only in what they teach but also, and maybe more importantly, in *how* they teach. A youth ministry that moves at the speed of the marketplace will most likely produce Christians who experience the faith as one more consumer item, one more piece of information to be downloaded and stored within an iPod rotation of ideas. My hope is that this book will inspire youth workers and parents to create youth ministries that are infused with the spirit and culture of prayer—ministries in which all our activities contain a sense of trust, gratitude, and compassion.

In recent years there has been an abundance of books on prayer and spiritual practice. It's as if the culture at large has realized its detachment from the sacred center of life and is now desperately grasping to find a way back home.[2] While I find the renewed focus on prayer encouraging, many of these books present lists of spiritual exercises that make prayer feel like either a systematic progression toward God or a catalog of gadgets that can be acquired, consumed, and then discarded.

With *Downtime*, I'm seeking to offer a different kind of prayer book—a book with the same rhythms and spirit I've experienced within my own life and glimpsed in the experiences of other seekers who have shared their inner lives with me. You'll see that this book—like prayer itself—is an intentionally unpredictable mixture of stories, ideas, methods, theological ruminations, meditations, Scripture passages, mystical quotes, and testimonies. My hope is that this book will stir up the Holy Spirit so youth workers, parents, and pastors might be inspired to discover creative, countercultural strategies for

---

[2] Many recent books on prayer are written from what I would call a "journalist's perspective," offering third-person reports on various exercises that Christians, past and present, have found helpful. Other books on prayer are more direct, written by people who have struggled to live a life of prayer and are now sharing from their experience. I find this second type of book far more valuable, because these writings not only give various methods of prayer but also communicate the spirit (and struggle) of prayer. See Daniel Wolpert's *Creating a Life with God;* Tilden Edwards' *Living in the Presence;* Marjorie Thompson's *Soul Feast;* and Basil Pennington's *Centering Prayer* or *Lectio Divina.* For some great insights on praying with youth, you may want to search old church libraries for copies of three books now out of print: Mark Link's *Experiencing Prayer* (Argus, 1984) and *Prayer Paths* (Tabor, 1990) and Betsy Caprio's *Experiments in Prayer* (Ave Maria Press, 1973).

giving young people the spiritual leisure necessary for knowing Jesus. My hope is that this book will encourage you to find ways to give young people the downtime they need to discover the prayers God is already praying within them.

Downtime is divided into two primary sections. In the first three chapters, I've offered some reflections on the nature of prayer and adolescence. Chapter 1 focuses on prayer and the need for downtime within youth ministry. Chapter 2 is a reminder of the theology, settings, and elements needed to invite young people into the life of prayer. Chapter 3 presents some of the capacities we pastors and teachers seek to embody as we invite young people into the life of prayer.

Section 2 describes a variety of prayer experiences, exercises, traditional prayer methods, settings, and strategies to help young people uncover the presence of God in their lives. This particular collection of exercises is in the spirit of what I'm calling "downtime." In other words, each exercise was chosen because of the way in which it embodies a sense of Sabbath—of rest, reflection, wonder, and meditation. These exercises seek to create a culture of listening and awareness that assists young seekers in making contact with the reality of God within and around them. In some ways it could be said that each prayer experience seeks to provide young people with the time and space needed to cultivate a life with God.

All the exercises in this book have been tried and tested by real youth ministers and real kids within a variety of rural, urban, ethnically and theologically diverse settings. (For interviews with participants see *Growing Souls: Experiments in Contemplative Youth Ministry*, Zondervan, 2007). During my years of research I observed and interacted with dozens of churches, spoke with hundreds of youth pastors, and read the prayer journals of youth, youth leaders, and pastors in order to gain some insight into the ways in which various prayer forms help young people attend to the spirit of God. Here I describe a variety of exercises that have been particularly helpful within my own ministry and the youth ministries I've studied.

Of course, the life of prayer is far more diverse (and personal) than the exercises I present in this book. Some readers might notice the absence of particular forms of prayer that are indispensable among followers of Jesus—such as intercessory prayers, prayers of confession, the Lord's Prayer, as well as other classical or biblical forms of prayer. Other readers may be surprised to find exercises that are rarely, if ever, included within books of prayer—

such as exercises that include sleep, befriending strangers, or traveling. Please note that my goal is not to present the breadth and depth of prayer forms within the Christian tradition.

If practiced over time, the exercises presented in this book will help churches provide a counter-cultural ministry for youth that is radical in the way it slows kids to the speed of God. I expect that as you read through this book you'll be inspired to design, modify, edit, and create your own settings for inviting youth into prayer. As you do, just remember that the method in which we pray with youth is never as important as the spirit in which we pray. Prayer grows in us not because of the technique or discipline in which we pray; it grows because of our willingness to open ourselves again and again, in times of darkness as well as in times of enlightenment, to the One who continues to love the world into being.

1 Holy Leisure and the Love of God

Most of the spiritual life is a matter of relaxing.

—BEATRICE BRUTEAU

In August 2003, I took a bus full of high school kids to the coastal dunes two hours north of San Francisco. This diverse group of young people, gathered from across the country, was spending the week exploring Christian prayer. Each morning 20 to 30 students congregated voluntarily in the seminary chapel for 20 minutes of silent prayer. An hour later, they were joined by the other 70 to 80 students and staff for a morning service that involved sung chants, intercessory prayer, readings from Scripture, and 10 minutes of silence. Mornings and afternoons were spent in plenary sessions exploring the life of Jesus and the mystical and praying tradition of the Christian church. Each day ended with vespers that again involved sung forms of prayer, Scripture, and long periods of silence.

Midway through the week, the leadership decided to see how far we could stretch the capacity of these young people for solitude and prayer. We loaded them into buses and drove them up the Northern California coast to the deserted expanse of the Bodega dunes. Gathered within the folds of the rolling sand, amid clusters of native grasses and twisting cypress trees, we talked to the students about the history of silence and solitude in the Christian tradition. We talked about the early desert Abbas and Ammas, the development of cloistered communities, and, in particular, the many times Jesus sought communion with God in lonely and deserted places. We asked the youth to see this time of silence and solitude not as a time of emptiness, but as a time of presence, a time to fully welcome God's love and companionship. As patches of fog from the Pacific Ocean drifted over us, we handed out journals and blankets and sent the young people out to pray.

I remember walking through the dunes carefully observing the praying teenagers. Some students sat atop mounds of sand, looking off to the horizon; others preferred low places, clefts and crevices stacked with driftwood. Some students lay on their backs, heads resting on their journals, watching gray shrouds of mist creep over the blue sky. Other students seemed oblivious to their surroundings, their heads bowed as they scribbled intently in their journals. As the hours passed some young people rolled themselves up in their blankets and closed their eyes, while others stood and meandered slowly toward the sea.

When the prayer time came to a close, I gathered the students together in small groups. "What was it like to pray?" I asked. "What were you like? What was God like?"

At the end of the week we asked the students to evaluate the retreat: "What was the most enjoyable aspect of our time together?" Despite volleyball, game nights, talent shows, karaoke, discussion groups, outings to San Francisco, and plenty of free time, the great majority responded, "The afternoon praying in the dunes." When I asked them why, they said things like, "I've never had that much unscheduled time before." Or "It was so peaceful to be told that it's okay to just rest with God." Or "My life is so stressful. I've never had time to just chill with God."

Eight months later I sat eating lunch with a 17-year-old girl from Cleveland, Ohio. Lauren had participated in the prayer week the previous summer. I told her how surprised I was that so many of her fellow students had found the extended time of prayer and solitude to be the highlight of the week. She listened, nodded her head knowingly, and then said, "Do you know what it's like to be a kid nowadays? There's no downtime." She sighed, turned and looked out the window, and then said quietly, as if she could feel the weight of her own words, "No downtime."

—❧—

We minister among young people who are trained to no longer see the presence of God in the world. We minister among budding consumers, people who have been told, "You are your appetites." We minister among people who are only allowed to live within a narrow band of their humanity, people imprisoned within the material world. We minister among kids whose worth is based on what Marcus Borg calls the three "As" of Western culture: Appearance, achievement, and affluence.[3] We minister among families and communities desperate for spiritual grounding. We minister among young people whose souls are

[3] Marcus Borg, *The Heart of Christianity* (Harper San Francisco, 2003), 116.

malnourished and depleted by a culture that worships, not the God of Jesus, but a God of our own making—an anxious God who condones human greed, violence, and self-absorption. We minister within a culture that is putting the souls of our young people to sleep. Consider how Hillary Hunt, a middle-aged shop steward for the AFSCME union, describes the formation of her own soul within the North American consumer culture:

> I know most of my fellow workers very well, and they are wonderful people. But many of us meet for a drink after work and talk about how dead we feel after a day in our offices. I sometimes remember what a lively little girl I was, how full of life and energy, and I wonder whatever happened to that girl. It's almost as if growing up is "coming down" from a high. Here I am now in a life where everything seems so mechanized and out of control. Sometimes I feel like I'm a zombie surrounded by zombies—everyone doing their assigned role, trying to fit in and be the way they are supposed to be, and even in the way that people talk to each other, it's so unreal and forced.[4]

[4] Michael Lerner, *The Left Hand of God* (Haper Collins, 2006).

The young people we serve will all too soon join Hillary Hunt in a world of restless "zombies" if they are not given the space and time to allow God to expand within them. What young people today are in desperate need of, what Hillary needed when she was full of "life and energy," is a way to stay in touch with the *source* of all life and energy. They need a way to stay grounded in God. Hillary, and the young people we serve, long for ways to bring their hopes, failures, and hungry spirits to the God who promises to give life in abundance.

How do young people stay in touch with their capacity for love and wonder? What keeps young people from becoming "zombies"—detached from the love and energy of God? How do we help young people carry the sorrows and joys that accompany life? We need to develop ministries that help young people not only absorb the stories and beliefs of the Christian faith but more importantly cultivate the heart and life of Jesus. We need to teach them to pray.

The ancient understanding of the word *pray* within the Christian tradition is "to rest." Any experience of rest requires a release—we have to set down our work, our agenda, our worry and activity. We can't remain in control when we sleep; we have to lie fallow, allowing our bodies to be renewed, receptive, and restored. The fact that Jesus spent long periods of time resting is one of the most over-looked aspects of his life.[5] He prayed and rested in the midst of suffering people. He prayed and rested in the midst of countless opportunities to do good. Why did Jesus rest? Why did he withdraw from crowds desperate for healing? We know from Scripture that Jesus rested in order to commune with God. For Jesus (even Jesus!), prayer was necessary in order to sustain and deepen his capacity for love. Prayer allowed Jesus to stay in touch with the deeper reality that God has always sought to express and embody in the world.

Like the students who spent an afternoon praying among the Bodega dunes, for young people today prayer is both a release from and resistance to the drivenness, overconsumption, and excessive activity that overwhelms their lives. Prayer gives young people permission to loosen the shoulders, relax the jaw, and soften the walls around the heart so God's love might make a way. Prayer, for most young people, is that increasingly rare opportunity to lie down in green pastures and rest beside still waters, despite the fear and worry that constantly assault us.

—∞∞—

[5] Another central aspect of Jesus' life that is often ignored by people in the United States is that Jesus was nonviolent. As Gandhi once said, "Why are Christians the only ones who don't understand that Jesus was nonviolent?"

Most Christians have relegated prayer to a type of service or religious duty that we perform—we pray for peace, we pray for courage, we pray for others. These prayers of intercession are very important and intrinsic to the Christian life. Intercession is one way in which we seek to partner with God in spreading God's healing love. However, this is only one aspect of our prayerful relationship with God. The foundation of prayer, the fundamental expression of our humanity, and the basic expression of our life in God is found in what the early monastics referred to as "holy leisure."

Holy leisure is not the idleness and laziness toward which Western society is so disdainful; nor is it the sort of grasping escapism promoted by the tourism industry. Leisure, in the spiritual sense of the word, describes "a condition of the soul."[6] It is a receptivity and gratefulness to the mystery and wonder of being alive in the world. Holy leisure is a spiritual attitude that seeks to behold the mystery of God's life and creation beneath the activities and roles we perform. It is an embodied trust in God. It is this holy leisure that we see in Jesus as he sleeps amid a stormy sea, teaches among resentful and antagonistic authorities, allows a repentant woman to wash his feet, or spends the night in solitude while people search anxiously for him.

[6] Josef Pieper, "Leisure as a Spiritual Attitude," *Weavings* (March/April 1993), Vol. VIII, Number 2: 9.

This holy leisure is the experience of faith. It is the way we allow ourselves to be enfolded by God's life and presence in the world. This kind of rest allows a person to be a person—rather than a function, a role, or a résumé of activities. Leisure is experiencing the gift of being human; it is a willingness to be overtaken by God's grace and mercy. Sacred leisure is coming home to oneself—with all the goodness and brokenness that we contain. This leisure is stepping out from the boundaries of our work and relational roles, and entering into the wide mystery of what it means to be alive and in the world. Leisure is the relief and contentment that arise when we finally stop all our striving and bargaining and simply allow our real selves (and the mixture of sin and holiness that is each of us) to come before the real God.

As children we fall into this state of holy rest naturally. We lie in the grass watching clouds form and dissipate; we swing on a front porch without any sense of time; we sit on our mother's lap allowing adult voices to roll over us like wind through the trees. The psalmist writes, "I have calmed and quieted my soul, like a weaned child with its mother; my soul is like the weaned child that is with me" (Psalm 131:2). It is in holy leisure that we experience *autarkeia*, the Greek word Paul uses to refer to a state of "contentment," "sufficiency," or "enough."

In the harried culture in which we live, young people are desperately yearning for holy leisure. They seek not the prayers of our faith as much as the disposition from which prayers arise. This state from which a young person is able to notice and receive God's prayer is what I am referring to as "downtime." Downtime is the holy leisure necessary to place ourselves at God's disposal. By *downtime*, I do not mean those moments when we escape, check out, or disengage from life. This kind of escape only increases our alienation and restlessness. I'm referring to a sort of *in*scape—a sinking down into the mysterious reality of life, a releasing of the unnecessary drivenness and amusements that cover up reality. In this sense, downtime is repentance—a returning to our natural dependence on and need for God.

In my experience it is often only when young people are given permission for "downtime" that they are able to step away from the anxious spirits that inhabit modern life and begin to discover and inhabit the presence of God. It is in these moments of spiritual rest and leisure that the communion of the Holy Spirit is received, and life within Christ becomes a sufficient reality. And it is in downtime that the false attachments of daily life are exposedand the love of God revealed and welcomed as the source of human freedom.

In a society gone mad with feverish activity, perhaps the gospel, the love of God, and the freedom of Jesus Christ are best communicated by inviting young people to rest and pray like Jesus. It's the life of prayer that will help young people resist the frantic consumption that afflicts us. It is prayer that will inspire young people to trust and follow God's hope. It is prayerful rest that will strengthen the spirits of young people so they will no longer fear difference or weakness or suffering. And it is prayer, much more than words, that will allow young people to feel the power and freedom of God's love.

When was the last time you allowed yourself downtime? Take a moment to withdraw from the busyness of your life. Find a quiet place where you won't be distracted—maybe it's outside, maybe it's behind a closed door. Then, like the young people on the Bodega dunes or the psalmist of Psalm 23, allow yourself to lie down. Spend a few moments just resting in God's love, in the same way you might enjoy the warmth of the sunlight on a beautiful day. If you feel sleepy, allow yourself to close your eyes, with an awareness that you are resting in God's love.

Consider these words from Meister Eckhart: "What keeps us alive, what allows us to endure? I think it is the hope of loving, or being loved. I heard a fable once about the sun going on a journey to find its source, and how the moon wept without her lover's warm gaze. We weep when light does not reach our hearts. We wither like fields if someone close does not rain their kindness upon us." In quiet reflection remember the last time you experienced love, like the sun's "warm gaze." Maybe it was from a child or a spouse or a friend, maybe it was from God. Take a moment to savor this experience of being loved. Now imagine that this love is a reflection of God's love for you. What is it like for you to bask and soak in God's love? What is your prayer as you take in this love?

If possible, plan to take one day this month to drive to a deserted place—a forest, a riverside, an empty field. Bring nothing except a journal and a blanket. Spend an afternoon with God in solitude and silence. What are you like after a day of solitude and prayer? What is God like on a day like this? Who would you be if you set aside time like this each month?

2 Trusting the Mystery

Prayer is not a matter of method or expertise but trust.
—BROTHER ROGERS

When I was 15 years old, a friend invited me to attend a youth ministry gathering at his church. We played games and ate snacks and then, at the end of the meeting, the parent who was in charge had us sit in a circle to close the meeting in prayer. Still horsing around, we gathered under the fluorescent lights, each taking a seat on one of the carpet samples. The leader asked us to quiet down, and then told us in a more stern voice that this was prayer and we needed to be respectful to God.

After the chatter subsided, we were instructed to bow our heads and close our eyes. It was so quiet and serious and counter to the previous two hours that I felt awkward and started to laugh. I covered my mouth but soon started shaking with giggles. I pinched my leg to make it stop, my eyes watered, but without warning bursts of air began to escape through my nose and hands like a deflating balloon. Startled, my friends opened their eyes and looked over at me. Of course, they found my suffering unbearably funny—and soon they too were holding their mouths and clenching their bellies as if undergoing a violent case of indigestion.

Meanwhile, the praying parent continued on in godly phrasing. Ignoring the growing restlessness, he raised his voice above the snorts and yips of the group. This only increased the tension. Our laughter unabated, the youth leader's prayer took a turn toward the tragic. In an obvious attempt to sober us, he began to describe various tragedies around the world—floods, fires, people lying in hospital beds with cancer, children maimed in car crashes. As his words became increasingly graphic, it was clear his prayer was directed toward us, not God.

Of course, none of this helped. Red-faced and sweating, my "hrmphs" and "eeeks" only got louder.

Determined to teach us piety, our leader refused to abandon the prayer. In his most forceful and pious voice he declared, "Lord, the world is a dangerous place. There may be a nuclear bomb headed right for our town at this very moment, about to obliterate all of us, and yet here we sit laughing at it all." Of course, this was too much. The thought that the Russians would target our small, economically depressed, uncultured, strategically insignificant town of Yreka, California, sent the whole group into fits of laughter. Unable to proceed our parent-leader abruptly ended the prayer and then with furrowed brow, admonished us about the holiness of God. I never returned to that youth group.

How do we invite young people to pray? How do we help young people discover the life of prayer without making it seem like another formal, unreal, strange, religious relic? How do we help youth pray when silence and prayer feel so odd and contrary to the hyperactive rhythms of the culture in which youth are formed? How do we help youth pray, when their own interior landscapes can feel awkward and foreign? How do we invite young people to allow their souls, minds, and hearts to be touched by God?

One reason prayer can feel difficult—for both adults and young people—is that prayer encourages an intimate truthfulness. Prayer draws out what Ann and Barry Ulanov call our "primary speech"—the words and expressions closest to our hearts.[7] In prayer, we are inspired to uncover all we know of ourselves, and more often, all we don't know. When we invite youth to pray, we invite them to allow their desire, suffering, and natural wonder to rise to the surface.

This is scary stuff. By the age of 13 most kids know that crying, passionate longing, and slack-jawed amazement are just invitations to ridicule. Youth learn through observation and experience that the real work of becoming an adult is to construct a hard, but attractive, shell—a barricade that keeps the soft and wild interior of a person hidden and protected. The culture teaches our young people to create hearts of stone rather than hearts of flesh. (See Ezekiel 11:19 and 36:26.)

Yet prayer is an invitation to become real, an invitation to shrug off the costumes and masks we wear and to reveal our true faces. The power of prayer, if "power" is the right word, is in its invitation to become unguarded, truthful, and vulnerable before God. If praying with youth is to be natural and honest instead of strange and otherworldly, there are a few things we need to keep in mind:

[7] *Primary Speech: A Psychology of Prayer* (John Knox, 1982)

Every Young Person Is a Mystery

Each young person we work with is a living, breathing mystery. It's easy to forget this, especially when the 15-year-old boy in your Sunday school class constantly falls asleep with bits of cereal drooling from the corner of his mouth.

Part of the work of ministry is remembering over and over that the young people in front of us are mysteries, carrying within them the divine spark, the sacred image of God. "You have made them a little lower than God, and crowned them with glory and honor," the psalmist reflects (8:5). As teachers we seek to treat youth in ways that reflect the same sense of wonder and dignity.

Of course, we sometimes wish our young people were less mysterious. We wish they would conform to the curriculum that has been carefully orchestrated to meet their developmental needs. We wish they would use their pens to fill out our meticulously crafted worksheets instead of trying to spear one another from across the room. But unfortunately for us, God has given youth great freedom. God has created every human being with great potential for love and cruelty, intelligence and ignorance, kindness and unending self-absorption, profound insights and stupid outbursts. We are each a mixture of light and shadow,

capable of imaginative acts of liberation as well as cal-
culated feats of destruction.

When we invite youth into prayer it's important to
remember they are made of the same yearnings and
sin and mystery and mundane habits we find within
ourselves. This is important to remember, because
young people are often seen as three-quarter humans
who don't deserve the same dignity and respect as
adults. We must also remember that young people
carry the light of God within their bodies, their words,
and their actions—even when we don't perceive it. In
fact, one of the great gifts we can offer young people
is time in the presence of someone who trusts their
capacity for holiness. We spend time with young people, trusting the light in their souls until they can trust
it themselves. It is this image of young people that we
carry within us that gives them the most encouragement for prayer. As Meister Eckhart understood:

> All beings are words of God,
> His music, His
> Art.
>
> Sacred books we are, for the infinite camps
> in our
> souls.

Every act reveals God and expands His Being.
I know that may be hard
to comprehend.

All creatures are doing their best
to help God in His birth
of Himself.

Enough talk for the night.
He is laboring in me;

I need to be silent
for a while,
worlds are forming
in my heart.[8]

When we enter a room of young people we are entering a room of "sacred books"—a room full of people who (whether they know it or not) are stretching and reaching for some kind of freedom, some kind of healing, some kind of truth that only God can give. We continue to trust that youth bear God's image, even when they snort with laughter, even when they keep goosing one another, even when they fall asleep, and even when their confor-

[8] Daniel Ladinsky, *Love Poems from God* (Penguin Compass, 2002), 112.

mity to the secular culture and their mimicking of adult avarice and greed is all we see.

Every Youth Prays

Eckhart says there are "worlds forming" within the heart of every young person. Some of these worlds seek to evoke the power and debauchery that so enamor our culture. Other worlds carry the dream and imagination of God. Youth, even youth from agnostic families, know something of God. Raised to believe in a world devoid of spirit and hope, a world reduced to matter and chaos, their hearts are still unable to quiet the whispers of the eternal: "For we do not know how to pray as we ought, but that very Spirit intercedes with sighs too deep for words" (Romans 8:26). When we engage youth in prayer, we trust that each of them has a prayer he or she is praying, although they might not be conscious of those prayers. Whether raised in a religious faith or not, every young person understands, instinctively, the human need to turn to the heavens and appeal for help, for guidance, for justice. Even the atheist shakes his fist at heaven and shouts (in the tradition of the Psalms), "Why me?" or watches the sun lay ribbons of purple and pink across the horizon and whispers, "My God..." We all pray—because we're all human and limited and broken and full of yearning.

We pray because we can't help but seek to connect with something more, something larger, something that responds, empowers, inspires, and justifies.

When we teach young people to pray, in part, we are helping them claim the prayers that are already stirring within them. "If we were to hear the soul's secret communication with God, we would be surprised," Brother Lawrence once suggested. This ongoing relationship between the depths of our own humanity and the depths of God is often ignored, covered over, and dismissed. And yet every time we invite young people to turn to God and pray, we are inviting them to hear and express that very intimate conversation that is already taking place between their own heart and the heart of God.

God Responds to Prayer

One of the most important aspects of teaching kids to pray is our own trust that God is actually present and responding—otherwise, prayer is simply an act of piety. We may not sense God's presence, but nevertheless we trust that God, even when hidden, is present and actively responding to our prayer. This is the essence of faith.

There's an old story about a pastor who goes to the hospital to see an aging parishioner who appears to be near death. Although the woman is incoherent and connected to various machines, he follows his normal routine for hospital visits. He sits beside the woman and reads Psalm 23 over her, then closes with a prayer for healing. Laying hands on the sickly woman, he prays, "Lord, I ask that you heal this woman from her illness..." Immediately, the woman sits up, rips off the oxygen mask, and shouts, "I'm healed!" She swings her legs over the side of the bed, unhooks the various wires and IVs, jumps up and runs through the hallways shouting, "Hallelujah, I'm healed! I'm healed!" The pastor, stunned and shaking, looks upward and says, "Don't you *ever* do that again!"

Many of us pray out of duty, hardly acknowledging or expecting that God is present and responding. Young people sense this. The truth, however, is that it is our trust, not our words, that allows God to move and breathe within us.

For years I led a project focused on prayer in youth ministry. Part of my work during that time was to visit congregations and observe the ways they were praying with their kids. I discovered that there were many things that could help facilitate or hinder prayer—but the one thing that seemed essential was trust. There had to be a sense that the youth leader or pastor trusted God (and the youth) in prayer.

What does it actually mean to trust God in prayer? It means we don't try to control it. It means we allow freedom in prayer. It means we come to God with patience and open hands. Without trust, any spiritual exercises and prayer methods we employ are useless.

Our prayer shows a lack of trust when it seems to allow no room for God. Sometimes our prayers with youth offer little silence or even patience within the prayer. The prayer seems to come from a script and is done as a duty, an obligatory act with little relevance or meaning. There is no sense that God might respond to our prayer, or that our prayer is in response to God's presence with us. This is the most common form of mistrust affecting the prayer life within churches. Soon prayer becomes a sacred monologue, rather than a living relationship. Making room for God means allowing silence, patience, solitude, and freedom in prayer. It means there is a sense of leisure—time and space for God to quicken within us.

Another mistake some churches and youth leaders make is allowing only adults and other trained leaders to pray. The message is simple: Prayer is an elite activity. God should be addressed only by those who have the language, training, and authority to pray. Although it is important for leaders to model prayer, when only the trained are permitted to pray, young people remain spiritually stunted and disempowered.

Our prayer with youth also becomes distorted when the language of our praying is directed to youth rather than to God. Like my experience as a teenager, this is didactic prayer intended to teach young people. It's prayer that seeks to be a model of right thinking and believing. God is used as a prop, a stand-in to help us teach the kids the right way to speak and behave. In this form of prayer we are not speaking to God as much as we are to the young people themselves. Meanwhile, the real God of Jesus is ignored and sidelined, while we model a praying life.

How helpful it would have been when I was a youth if the leader had laughed along with us in prayer. He would have reduced much of the tension if his prayer simply acknowledged how we were feeling, instead of ignoring or pushing it away: "God, we can't help but laugh. [Leave some space for kids to laugh.] Prayer seems so strange and quiet. But we know you welcome our giggles and laughter as much as our tears..." For some reason many prayers in churches and youth groups ignore the truth of our situation. Such prayers often take on strange language and phrasing, as if we expect kids to set aside who they are and pretend to be someone else as they pray. Often it is prayer that speaks only of spiritual things, ignoring the realities of our current situation and the good news that God is within and among us.

A number of years ago I was the keynote speaker for a suburban church youth group that was building homes for the poor along the U.S.-Mexico border. During the week we lived in an orphanage. The families living near the orphanage were often hungry, and lived in homes made of tarps and corrugated tin. The children in the orphanage suffered from many emotional and physical problems. Yet each night when we gathered for worship, the suburban pastor would pray for the salvation of the young people. Not once did he offer prayers for the orphans or the hungry families, nor did he acknowledge the disillusionment and suffering of the young people from his church as they encountered poverty. When I asked the pastor about this, he said, "I can't do anything about the poverty. My job is to point these kids to Jesus." And so night after night the pastor created an unreal situation. In the midst of suffering and poverty he prayed that kids would commit their lives to Jesus, ignoring the ways Jesus was seeking to reach out to the young people through the orphans, the struggling families, and their own disillusionment and heartbreak. The pastor's unspoken message to the young people of his church was, "God has nothing to do with these suffering people or your own painful confusion. God has nothing to do with what you see and experience. God's concern is that you get to heaven."

My studies found that prayer is relegated to the margins of many youth ministry programs. What do we communicate about the presence of God when we rarely turn our attention to God? Often the message is that we would rather talk about or serve God than actually listen to or spend time with God. There's a sense that God isn't really necessary to the Christian life—so we pray less and less, we listen less and less, and over time prayer (and God) becomes a strange archaic practice. But when our prayer life dies or diminishes, we suffer. Churches become dry, full of activity and words that are uninspired, disconnected from the spring of God's Spirit. Pastors and youth directors begin to feel that they, and not the Holy Spirit, are the driving force within their churches and ministries. Young people learn that the Christian life is about doing good or holy works for a God who is distant, demanding, and increasingly irrelevant to the concerns of everyday life.

When we invite youth to pray, we are inviting them to turn and acknowledge the presence of God. In this way our method soon becomes our message. Just inviting youth to pray in openness and trust communicates something about the nature of God and a young person's capacity to participate in Jesus' mission of love. The more we pray with young people, the more we communicate the reality and potential of God within all of life.

Those of us who minister with youth must ask ourselves, "When do I allow God to participate in the ministry?" When there is little prayer within our ministries, often it is because we have little trust in God. Why is this? Maybe we've felt betrayed by God? Maybe we've had experiences where God seemed unresponsive to our prayer? Maybe, deep down, we feel it's up to us, not God, to bring kids into faith. Our images of God will affect the way we pray with young people. If we don't trust that God is available and responsive to our prayers, then we will find lots of other pressing activities to engage in, leaving prayer as an exotic practice best left to nuns and mystics.

It Is God Who Teaches Prayer

One of the most overlooked aspects of prayer is that prayer is a learning process. In prayer we are learning who we are; we are learning how to live our lives; we are learning to let go of our sin and fear and to trust Divine Love. Prayer is a place of deep transformation; it is a school of spiritual living in which God serves as teacher. God tutors each of us uniquely in the ways of prayer. Sometimes God draws us to prayers of intercession; other times we find ourselves filled with prayers of confession and healing; other times prayers of thanksgiving and gratitude spill out of us; and there are yet other moments when God calls us to be silent and attentive. As ministers to young people, we must recognize that we are not the real teachers of prayer. It is God who teaches and directs the prayer of young people. It is the Holy Spirit that kindles prayer. It is Jesus who shows us how to pray. And it is God, the Creator, who holds and responds to our prayer.

This truth was brought home to me when I was asked to teach contemplative prayer to a group of young people at a conference in Colorado. During one workshop I invited the young people to practice a form of contemplative prayer in which they were invited to simply sit and rest in silence with God. After only a minute or so, I noticed a young woman drawing with pencil and paper. I quietly walked over to this student and reminded her this was a time just to sit in silent communion with God—"There will be time to draw later." She nodded her head quietly, set down her pencil, and closed her eyes. A few minutes later I heard some rustling and looked over to see the same young woman, this time with her back to me, hunched over her paper, drawing. I refrained from saying anything, but after the workshop ended I approached the young woman and said, "I asked you to put your paper away because I wanted you to experience silent prayer. Rarely do we take the chance to just be quiet and listening before God." The young woman listened politely, then said, "I really did try to just sit there, but this image just kept coming to me over and over. I let it go, like you instructed, but it just was so powerful that I felt like God wanted me to get it on paper."

She showed me the picture of a small group of people—some children and adults, shaded in various colors—standing around a cross. As I was looking at the picture another youth leader, a middle-aged Caucasian woman stood by me and looked at the picture. "When did you draw this?" the woman asked the young student. "During the silent prayer," she replied sheepishly. Tears began to fill the eyes of the youth leader. She asked if she could hold the picture. The young woman nodded her head. The youth leader held the picture tenderly, taking in the penciled image as if it were a sacred icon. After a few moments she explained, "My husband is Chinese American. We have three adopted children, all of whom are African American. Our church and denomination are almost entirely white. Last night my husband said he doesn't feel the church is welcoming to people of color. During the prayer I was asking God to give me some encouragement to stay in the church. Your picture of all these people with different shades of skin holding hands around a cross feels so encouraging. It is an answer to prayer."

When the group gathered again that night, I told this story and reminded them, and myself, that God is the one who leads us in prayer. I told the students that when we have a choice between following a prayer method or the Holy Spirit, we should do what the young student did, and follow the Holy Spirit.

No matter how much we desire it, we cannot make young people pray, nor can we make God respond. We must remember over and over that we don't control the spiritual lives of teenagers: Our role is to create a place of trust and safety where young people feel safe enough to express their prayers. No matter how much we try, we cannot do a young person's praying for them. All we can do is invite them to listen and trust that God is present and attentive. We can only create settings where a young person feels free enough to turn to God and say, "Here I am."

—◦◦◦—

Twenty-five years after my laughing fit as a teenager in youth group, I sat in a different circle of praying people. This was a circle of spiritual directors. We'd spent the day praying and discerning the Spirit's leading on a new initiative we were hoping to undertake within mainline congregations. It was the end of the day and all of us were feeling tired. As the facilitator of the group, I invited us to hear the daily Scripture, followed by 10 minutes of silent meditation and then we would close the time by reciting the Lord's Prayer together. I read the Scripture, we sat in silence, and then I started to lead the group in the Lord's Prayer: "Our Father, who art in heaven, hallowed be thy name. Our daily bread, our kingdo..." I've led churches and groups in reciting the Lord's Prayer hundreds of times, but for some reason I messed up the second line—"Thy kingdom come, thy will be done"—causing the whole group to stumble.

I noticed the mistake, but couldn't remember what was next. I faltered, searching for words, and soon stopped speaking altogether, hoping someone in the group would pick it up and lead us. Instead the whole group fell into an abrupt silence. It seemed I'd thrown the whole group off, and we were all equally confused as to the next line of the prayer. Eyes closed, we all waited for someone to continue the prayer.

Eventually, one brave soul tried, "As we give our bread…" This was also ridiculously wrong. I started to lose it. The idea that this group of highly educated pastors and spiritual directors, people who hoped to reform churches through prayer and spiritual direction, could not even recite the Lord's Prayer, struck me as insanely funny. I started to laugh, which caused the people next to me to giggle. Finally, my friend Frank burst out in great guffaws until tears ran down his face. For at least five minutes great waves of laughter swept over the group. When we finally regained our composure, someone sighed and said, "Dear God, thank you for the laughter and for the lesson in humility. We trust that even when we can't remember the words, you know and hear our prayer." To which we all enthusiastically responded, "Amen."

This is the trust and honesty I needed as a young person in prayer. And it is the same truthfulness, humility, and faith we seek to embody every time we say to kids, "Let us pray…"

———❧———

Take out some crayons or colored pens and paper. In prayerful quiet ask the Holy Spirit to help you create an image of what is taking place when you pray with young people. You may find that a recognizable image comes to you as you pray and draw, or you might simply gain a sense of how God is present to you and the youth as you pray together. What do you notice in this exercise? What is your role in helping youth to pray?

Similar to the exercise above, using paper and colors in prayer, see if you can discover the image of God you carry right now. Then take some time to express your image of young people. What do these images have to teach you about your role in ministry?

Spend some time in prayerful reflection over your own adolescence. What was your prayer life as a teenager? What settings, words, people, experiences helped you pray?

What kind of church, ministry, or mentors did you need as a teenager to deepen your love for God?

3 The Teacher

We're trying to create a situation where God can walk through the room.

—BONO

Jesus teaches prayer by praying. We do the same. We pray among, and on behalf of, young people—trusting that it is our *life* of prayer, more than our words and teachings *about* prayer, that will communicate God's love. In my experience, it is a praying person who invites others to pray, more than a particular method or teaching. "If you alone find peace, thousands around you will be saved," St. Seraphim once counseled. And so we seek to free God's life within us, allowing the peace of God to course through our bloodstream so we might carry this peace into the lives of young people.

The best preparation for teaching kids to pray is for us to spend time in prayer ourselves. The time you spend in prayer isn't selfish or frivolous; rather it is deeply connected to the ministry and life of the young people you serve. Few things have caused me more tension and pain than having to observe kids being led in some form of prayer by a youth leader who is unaccustomed to prayer. There is a falseness, a sense of going through the motions, that undercuts all the religious language and gives a sense that prayer is some form of holy pretending.

Here are some of the ways in which we become teachers of prayer:

Tend your own flame. A good youth minister keeps the sacred core burning within. To do this we need to give ourselves space and time. Like Jesus we need inner and outer spaces that are deserted, places where we can escape the constant worry, envy, self-abuse, and temptations our culture feeds on. If possible, find a place outside: A backyard, a creek bed, the hillside behind a housing development, an abandoned bench on the church grounds. If you can't go outside, find a place indoors where you won't be disturbed—an empty church classroom, the sanctuary, a cleaning closet. Try not to use your office as a prayer space—too many temptations and interruptions.

When you find a place to pray you might begin by lying down. Lie down on the grass, on the bench, on the carpeted floor of the classroom. Lie down and open yourself before God. Hand over all the desires and disappointments you carry to God. Release whatever struggle, shame, or hardship lies within you. Put your hands over your own heart, and then surrender yourself to love.

As you seek to deepen your prayer life, it might be helpful to add some variety and creativity to your time of prayer. Draw. Journal. Write your prayers in the dirt. Float your prayers down the creek. Like human courtship, you may find different settings and activities help stir your passion for God. Block time in your calendar to take dates with God. Go walking, eat good food, watch the sunset, sing, write letters—simply enjoy your time with God. Let this time fill, heal, and inspire you.

Over time you might discover a way of praying that feels natural. A time of day. A sacred place. A rhythm and method of prayer. I've found it helpful in my own prayer time to read a piece of Scripture (often based on the lectionary), then have a little silence and see how the words settle in. I reflect on the Scripture with an awareness of God, seeing what God might want to bring to my attention. Eventually I rest in the silence, just breathing in the quiet and truth of God.

The important thing in practicing prayer is to remember that you are not trying to get anywhere. This isn't a self-improvement project. You're not trying to gain anything—you're simply trying to remember that everything you need is already here.

Pray with others Perhaps the best way to help young people learn to pray is by providing them not just with a praying teacher, but also with a praying community. "When two or three are gathered in my name, there am I also," Jesus said. I've found that a praying community helps me keep accountable to my own life in God and reminds me that the work of ministry is a communal work. People who spend time in prayer are familiar with and unruffled by the boredom, doubt, distractions, and resistance that can be present in prayer. There is a trust present in people who pray, a trust that God is moving and working even when they are distracted or restless.

Much of my work in youth ministry has been training and encouraging churches to provide young people with a group of adults who pray for and with kids. (See *Contemplative Youth Ministry: Practicing the Presence of Jesus.*) Nothing is more encouraging to a person's spiritual life than being immersed within a community of prayer. Identify the praying people in your church and ask them to come early and pray with you before a youth gathering. Maybe there are parents or other adults who volunteer with kids who could join you for 30 minutes of prayer. These need not be times of just intercessory prayer. Sometimes it's encouraging to just sit in silent prayer with people before engaging in ministry, allowing God (often in hidden ways) to reorder our priorities, heal our insecurities, and give us guidance for the ministry. A group of people seeking God's presence is irresistible to the Holy Spirit.

Another way to be encouraged by others in prayer is to read the writings and biographies of praying people. Read Thomas Merton, Dorothy Day, Teresa of Avila, Howard Thurman, Francis of Assisi, Henri Nouwen, Mother Teresa, and others. Remember that these people were just as broken and full of anxiety and shame and yearning and sin as we all are. Read their prayers and struggles. Let them encourage and accompany you in your ministry with youth.

Pray for youth. One item in the job description of every youth worker should be, "Pray for the youth in our community." Take time to pray for your students. Hold them in prayer. Pray their worries, their fears, their dreams and yearnings. Pray for them after classes and meetings. Say their names and see their faces in prayer. As you spend time holding these kids before God, you will begin to see them and care for them as God does.

Pray among youth. Sometimes it can be a struggle to keep an abiding awareness of God during all the time we're among young people. Seek to let every encounter with youth draw you into prayer. Let their faces be like the bells of the church that call people toward God. Just as the 17th-century monk Brother Lawrence practiced an "interior glance," looking and noticing God with the eyes of his heart as he washed dishes and swept the floor, so too can we look over and become aware of God's presence as we load the church van, play basketball with a group of 12-year-old girls, or organize kids in discussion groups. When we're among kids, we look and see Christ among us—we acknowledge Christ's love and presence and then do our work with open and joyful hearts.

Pray with youth. It's good to have regular occasions for prayer within youth gatherings. Pray at the beginning of meetings. Pray before meals. Pray when someone expresses worry or hurt. Pray to close a gathering. Every time we pray we communicate something of God. Be sure not to use these prayer times to teach or impress, instead really turn to God and become aware of the longing that God is stirring within you and the young people you serve.

Most of all, really pray so young people can hear the work of God within you. When we pray with youth it's important that we give space for them to pray. Just as Jesus invited his friends to pray with him, we too invite kids to turn and pray, trusting they'll find their way to God. Every time you pray with kids, make room and time for them to encounter God. Leave silence in prayer, remembering that silence is God's first language. Invite kids to pray their own prayer within them. Try to let go of worries about whether a prayer exercise is "working" and trust that God is at work. If there are youth who become disruptive, speak the truth in love. Call them back to prayer using an economy of words.

When inviting youth to pray it's important to have an informal and "experimental" tone, especially if you have unchurched kids or kids who are not familiar with silence or prayer. The more informal and relaxed you are, the less nervous (and giggly) the kids will be. In setting the tone for an exercise, you might say something like, "We're going to try an experiment in prayer. It may or may not be the way in which you're used to praying. You may even feel a little strange or uncomfortable, but I want to ask you to give it a try to see what happens. God can surprise us sometimes and show up in ways we don't normally expect."

When we're trying new forms of prayer with young people it's important to describe what we're doing before we pray. Youth and adults get anxious and nervous when they don't know what's happening, especially when it involves silence. So if you're leading a prayer that involves silence or meditation make sure everyone understands how the exercise will proceed. I've found it's particularly important to let people know how long the silence will last. Otherwise kids will look around and wonder if the leader has fallen asleep. If prayer involves silence I try to help young people see that silence is actually a very familiar activity, something we've all experienced when we stop speaking and listen attentively to a friend.

It's also important when you're inviting young people into an unfamiliar form of prayer to acknowledge the common difficulties we face in prayer. I often say something like, "Sometimes when we pray it's difficult to focus—our minds are moving too fast, we're tired, or maybe this just isn't the best way for us to pray. That's okay. Don't get stressed if you're having a hard time with this particular form of prayer. Just simply say within yourself, 'God, I want to be with you right now,' and let that be enough."

One of the greatest blocks to prayer is our expectation of what should happen in prayer. It's important to remind kids that even monks who've spent years in silent prayer commonly experience periods where they can't focus, their minds distracted and wandering. If we don't mention difficulties, people often begin to judge themselves harshly: "Nothing happened in my prayer...I can't do this. I'm just not spiritual."

It's important for young people to understand there is no "right" way to experience prayer. Sometimes in prayer we get ideas or insights that seem to come to us from God. Sometimes we may have a feeling of God's compassion or kindness. Sometimes an image emerges in prayer. Sometimes there is a physical sensation. I tell kids that most of my experience in prayer is struggling to trust and be present to God—no images, words, insights—just a sense of trying to be myself before God.

We can't make young people pray, we can only invite. One way in which our invitation becomes appealing is by removing the needless anxieties and inhibitions that can prevent a young person from seeking God.

Trust. Before you lead any prayer experience with youth it's important to remember that the ministry, the young people, and you, yourself are enfolded within the loving arms of God. Sometimes when I'm particularly anxious I pray, "God, this is your ministry and these are your kids. Help me to be an instrument of your peace." Before any youth gathering or prayer exercise, we offer ourselves and our ministries to God and then trust that God is holding the prayer and the ministry.

There's a strange paradox in seeking to teach youth to pray. As a youth pastor or adult leader, your own prayer encourages, teaches, and even makes a way for the praying life of your students. At the same time, the spiritual life of your students does not rely on you. We must remember that the kids we work with belong to God, not us. God is the real spiritual teacher. God is the one seeking to do the work of prayer within them. God has been stirring, hearing, responding to, and encouraging the life of prayer within our students long before we encountered them.

So pray lightly.

There is no weight on your shoulders.

The souls of your students rest in God.

When we invite young people to pray, we are inviting them to make contact with the deep swells and tides within their own souls. Prayer, for the most part, is simply allowing kids to slow down and notice the life of God within them.

Within the mystical tradition one of the images of how God comes alive in us is the story of young Mary bearing Jesus from her own body out into the world. In a similar way God seeks to be born within the heart of every young person. As youth leaders we are called to be witnesses and, further, to be mid-wives to this spiritual birthing.

I've never received training as a midwife, but I have accompanied my wife through the birth of each of our three children. When Jill was laboring with our first son, I played soft music, dimmed the lighting, and lay next to my wife breathing with her and timing her contractions. At times I walked with her, rubbed her back, and brought her water and ice chips. I drove her to the hospital, helped communicate with the hospital staff, and spent a lot of time holding her hand, waiting, watching, worrying, and praying—hoping and trusting that she and our baby would be all right.

I was less involved with the birth of our second child. Jill knew what she was doing and asked me to keep the hospital staff at bay while she labored alone in the shower. After a couple of hours she asked for half a piece of gum. Other than that I stood outside the shower waiting, watching, worrying, and praying.

The labor for our third child was long and difficult. Jill refused medication for all three births, yet the hospital staff kept insisting that she take some form of pain medication. (We later learned that the nurses on duty that day had never observed a natural birth and didn't know what to expect.) During her labor Jill needed me to protect her space, to keep the anxious nurses at a distance so she could focus on the labor. I engaged in arguments with the hospital staff, pushed aside IVs filled with pain medication, escorted nurses out of our room, and continually communicated to the managing doctor that I had full trust in Jill.

I play the same role in the spiritual lives of young people. Most of my job is to trust that each young person is giving birth to his or her own life in God. This is actually a very natural process when young people are given room, time, teaching, and spiritual companionship. Sometimes young people need me to design and direct exercises that help them pray; other times my role is simply to keep the space open and clear of distractions. Most importantly young people need me to trust their capacity for God, keeping the anxiety of the culture at bay.

Our role in nurturing the prayer lives of young people is similar to the role I've played during the birth of our children. We create the setting, protect the space, engage various exercises, offer encouragement and support, listen, respond, pray, and then wait—knowing our youth are in God's hands, not ours.

When you think of "praying people" in your life, who comes to mind? What are some of the qualities of these people? What do they communicate about life with God? What aspects of these people would you like to emulate in your own life?

Look through your calendar and block out times for daily prayer. If your schedule is full with family and work, try finding little spaces like the drive home from work, a walk to a bus stop, lying in bed at night. Try to set aside time to pray each day and then notice how it affects your life and ministry.

Sometimes what keeps us from prayer is some internal resistance. We may have anger, disappointment, guilt, or shame that keeps us from spending time with God. Take out a piece of paper and make a diagram of your heart. (This doesn't have to look like the traditional valentine heart; it could be a series of images, a building, etc.) Where are the places in your heart that long for prayer? What places in your heart are resistant, angry, or doubtful? Place your hand on eac h of these places and pray for them. Pray with compassion for those places in your heart that are resistant to God. Pray with encouragement for those places within you that enjoy dwelling in God's presence.

Prayers and Exercises

4 Withdraw

But he would withdraw to deserted places and pray.
—LUKE 5:16

All human beings need retreat, some kind of withdrawal from our daily lives, in order to live. Life is hard, and its sufferings are only compounded by the way in which we attempt to manage it. Many Americans try to stop the hustle of our lives by withdrawing into television, computers, or other forms of amusement. Watching television often isn't a form of retreat as much as an abandonment of the self—we use television to escape, to vacate our lives, or to "veg out" (reducing our brain function to that of a brussels sprout). Withdrawing, for many of us, means handing ourselves over to the lights and sounds of flashing screens.

There is nothing wrong with the desire to withdraw from life. God knows we all need a break from the constant activity of our lives from time to time. That's why we're commanded to take a Sabbath, a rest, a retreat, a "down day" in which we step away from the habits and routines of human life. Jesus had to withdraw in order to pray, and young people are no different. What young people need, however, isn't an escape into amusing (or even spiritual) distractions as much as a retreat into the depths of their humanity, into the wider landscape of their inner being, into the reality of their life with God.

Stopping and withdrawing is a necessary practice within the spiritual life. When we pray with young people, we are inviting them to stop and enter God's time and God's space. In many monastic communities bells are rung at various times throughout the day calling the various members of the community to cease their activity, fall on their knees, and pray. I've been on retreat at a monastery where I watched men in kitchens, in fields, in gift stores and libraries suddenly stop their work, fall to their knees, and open their hearts to God.[9] This break from activity helps them keep perspective; it keeps the members of the community in touch with the reality of God's

[9] For an experience of this kind of daily prayer, see *Into Great Silence*, (Zeitgeist Films, 2006) a documentary set within a Trappist monastery high in the Swiss Alps. Without soundtrack or commentary, the film documents the silence and prayer the men living at the monastery seek to embody.

life within and around them. Stopping is Sabbath-keeping—God's compassionate commandment that frees us from our activity and striving, we might receive and enjoy our life with God.

Stopping relieves us of the trance of modern life. Stopping helps us keep a certain detachment from the "tyranny of urgency" that blinds and sickens our culture. Every time I minister with kids, I try to break the trance of consumer living. I try to break this trance by being present and listening. I try to break this trance by being real and honest. I try to break the trance by asking kids to see, hear, and feel what's happening in the world. Most often, I seek to break the trance by helping youth slow down. "Forgive them, Lord, for they know not what they do," is Jesus' diagnosis of humankind; the remedy is to be present and aware of our life and God's life in the world. This is prayer.

How do we help kids withdraw into prayer? How do we help them slow down to the speed of God? How do we help them cease their frenzied business and sink down into the rhythm and time clock of God?

Disconnect

It's difficult for kids to connect to God in prayer when they are caught in a constant stream of electronic connection to the information, relationships, and activity provided by the digital world. In Jesus' day, withdrawing into prayer was as simple as walking to the top of the nearest hill. Nowadays you have to ensure that your hilltop has poor cell phone reception. Helping kids stop and withdraw into prayer means providing a refuge from the portable video games, music devices, handheld computers, phones, and all the other personal electronics that can fracture a young person's attention.

In youth gatherings I not only have kids turn off their various devices, but also ask them to leave their gadgets at the door. This helps remove the temptation to check email, text message a friend, or see if anyone has called. When I first began this practice, it met with a lot of resistance from kids who felt they could not live without their devices, or worried the devices would be lost or damaged. With humor and much persistence I had to explain over and over that in order to discover God we needed to be in the present moment with one another and with God. Over time the youth began to pride themselves on going two whole hours(!) without their cell phones and began to monitor, on their own, the use of gadgets within the group.

Change the Scenery

Some of my friends in youth ministry create youth rooms that try to emulate the culture, with walls covered in posters of Christian rock bands or athletes with inspirational verses. I've found it more helpful to create youth rooms that speak not only to the energy of young people but also to the souls of young people. Often this means creating a space that invites spiritual reflection and prayer, one that draws young people into a different sense of space and time—so prayer seems a natural activity, rather than an abrupt shift from the speed and pace of the culture.

This was brought home to me when I visited Jeremy, a friend was running a youth ministry at a Lutheran church outside Chicago. The church had recently gone through a period of growth and decided to move its morning worship and adult Sunday school classes from the sanctuary to the church youth room and gymnasium. The youth group was now meeting in the former sanctuary. I attended the youth group meeting one Sunday night and was struck immediately by the beauty of the sanctuary. It was a simple wood interior with a handmade cherry wood chancel, high beam ceilings, soft lighting, and simple stained-glass windows. The pews had been removed and floor pillows and soft padded chairs were placed in a circle in the middle of the sanctuary. I watched as kids lowered their voices and slowed their activity as they entered the sanctuary/youth room. It was clear that the sanctuary itself communicated a different sense of time and space.

After a typical youth meeting of games, Bible study, and discussion, the students gathered in a circle for evening prayer. The prayer was led by various students who sang responses, invited silent confession, read Scripture, and facilitated silent meditation. I had rarely witnessed such a large group of kids leading and participating in such a long period of prayer. When the service ended, the lights were turned on and I noticed 10 or 15 adults at the perimeter of the room. Later Jeremy told me these adults were church members who were attracted to the evening prayer time and now came on their own to participate.

The next chapter will say more about the need for and power of sacred space.

Live at the Speed of Humanity

Not only does the space affect how young people enter into awareness of God, so does the way we approach time. Prayer is giving our attention to God. We all know what it's like to try to talk with someone when we feel harried. Often we only half-listen and say things we don't mean. The same is true in prayer. Helping kids pray means creating youth gatherings that move at a human pace. When kids arrive, we slow down and look at them, listen to them, set aside our agendas in order to address their questions and needs. A friend of mine who led a youth ministry in Texas often started youth group with a leisurely dinner. Kids were encouraged to sit and talk and eat family style. Brent felt this kind of start to youth group formed kids in the kind of ease and significance of relationship needed in prayer.

Center Down

When we actually lead kids in prayer, it's important to help them not only cease their activity, but also draw inward into God. In the praying tradition this is referred to as "recollection" or (as my Quaker friends would say) "centering down." All of us need simple ways to help us center ourselves in God. We need ways to push off from the surface of our lives and sink into God's mercy and grace. In youth ministry centering exercises can be particularly important if you're transitioning from a game or other high-energy activity. Again, space can help prepare kids for prayer. In one youth group I led, I walked the kids slowly from the basement to the chapel every time we prayed. This change in space often did wonders to help kids settle down and turn their attention to God. Here are some other ways to help young people quiet their hearts and minds and turn their attention to God:

- Singing simple prayer songs or chants like the music from the community at Taizé, France, can help young people open their attention to God.[10] Listening to music that is prayerful in nature, either instrumental or sacred, can also ready kids for prayer.

- I've also found it helpful to use guided images as a way of readying young people to draw their hearts toward God. You might say something like, "As we begin, close your eyes and imagine that Jesus has just walked into the room. He smiles at you, a look of recognition on his face, then quietly takes a seat next to you. For a few moments imagine that Jesus is sitting next to you, patient and waiting to pray."

- Another guided meditation invites youth to journey into the depths of their selves: "Before we begin, I'd like you to imagine that you are walking down a staircase that begins in your mind and winds slowly down to your heart. Take a few moments to imagine walking this staircase, leaving all the many worries and thoughts behind, slowly descending into a secret room or chapel within your heart where God waits to pray with you."

[10] "Music from Taizé" GIA Publications Inc., 7404 S. Mason Ave., Chicago, IL 60638.

- I sometimes invite students to a time of prayer by asking them to focus on the very simple act of breathing: "As we begin I want to invite you to close your eyes and simply notice your breathing. Take a moment to imagine the air in the room is filled with God's light and God's love. For the next few minutes just pay attention to your breathing, imagining with each in-breath that you are breathing in God's love, and with every out-breath you are releasing every distraction, every anxiety, every tension and resistance to God."

- Before beginning a prayer exercise invite students to ask God to help them in their prayer. I might say, "Let's take a few moments to offer this time to God. For the next few moments, dedicate this time and place to God, asking God to help us pray. What is it you're feeling as we begin our time of prayer? What is getting in the way of your ability to pray? Take a few moments to give these things to God."

A friend of mine has a small herd of sheep. When the weather turns cold, he keeps them in a barn. In the morning he goes to the barn and leaves food in a trough on one side of the room. One night he came home from work and heard the sheep bleating. This was unusual, so he went down to investigate. When he opened the door, he found the sheep crowded in a corner, their backsides to the trough, baying with hunger. He looked over at the feed trough and noticed it was still full. My friend then walked over and, one by one, turned the sheep around and led each one to the trough.

Jesus' image for humanity is "sheep without a shepherd." Sheep are not very bright.[11] They are herd animals, manipulated by fear and groupthink. When we minister with youth (or any group of people) we are working with people who have been strongly formed by the rhythms and values of mainstream consumer culture. Within this culture the Christian life appears unproductive, useless, and "boring" (or lifeless). This is what happens to youth who have been herded into believing real life is found within the pumping sounds, erotic images, and caffeinated drinks of the marketplace.

To lead youth to the real food and drink of prayer, often the first step is to help young people stop. We have to make a clean break from the regular speed and activity they're accustomed to. We must help them turn and notice the hidden life of God. Help-

---

[11] My great-grandfather was a street entertainer in Italy. He was poor and often used common farm animals in his performances. The one animal he refused to work with was sheep. According to my grandfather, my great-grandfather often said, "They are unteachable because they remember nothing."

ing teenagers pray not only involves creating sacred space, it also means creating empty, open space where God (and our own emerging lives) can be sensed and received. This is what Jesus continually sought out—empty, lonely, deserted places, places unaffected by the worry and demands of culture, places hospitable to God.

Like stepping into a cool stream of water, this kind of withdrawing into God leaves kids renewed and refreshed and gives them a sense of the real life God seeks to offer them. It is this kind of retreat that is needed if human beings are to be healed from the mindless habits of speed and accumulation that leave so many of us agitated, angry, and unsatisfied.

5 Create Space

Have them make me a sanctuary, so that I may dwell among them.
—EXODUS 25:8

One night in college while I was at a movie with my girl-friend, my roommate and a group of friends snuck into my apartment, lit candles, put on a Miles Davis album, and set out cookies and hot chocolate for us to find when we returned from our date. They created an intimate setting that would invite Jill and me to deepen our relationship. We do the same in youth ministry. Youth directors are matchmakers; we facilitate relationships of love between God and young people. Much of our work is about creating an environment that encourages young people to open their hearts to God. Because prayer is intimate and relational, I often rely on the very techniques used in romancing a relationship between two people—I light candles, play soft music, create a space that has beauty and privacy—all the while seeking to fan the flames of love between young people and their Creator.

Sometimes just being in a sacred place draws a young person's prayer to the surface. When my daughter, Grace, sees a park or playground, she gets excited. She jumps and hops and points and smiles. A playground draws up excitement and a sense of play in her. In the same way, I've taken my youth groups to cathedrals and other sacred places that seemed to stimulate prayer within them. There was no need for teaching—just the beauty, the history, the sacred art, the silence, and the spiritual weight of the many people who had prayed in that space made us vulnerable to God. Spaces can open us, calm us, or agitate us; they can warm, frighten, or delight us. Temples, deserts, seas, and mountains were the places Jesus seemed to find most conducive to prayer. What places draw you to prayer?

Take time to visit a sacred cathedral, chapel, or another place where people gather to pray. Notice the lighting, the aesthetics, and the visual aids to prayer. In my observations of youth groups and churches, space is the most neglected aspect when leading youth in prayer. I've suffered through many restless youth group prayer gatherings in which youth were distracted and inhibited from prayer because the space was cluttered or institutional, glaring with fluorescent lights and invaded by ambient noises.

When I invite youth to pray I often dim the lighting. I clear out the furniture. I seat kids in a circle with a candle, cross, or other sacred focal point. Sometimes I play meditative music, especially if I need to cover over competing sounds. It's nice to have comfortable seats or pillows for extended periods of prayer. Since prayer often touches the most private and personal aspects of who we are, it's important to make a place of prayer open and simple, so kids can feel safe to turn their hearts over to God. Often it's helpful to allow students to create a space for prayer, so they'll take ownership and feel more connected to the space.

The spaces we create can help youth slow down, stop, and pray. I once took a group of kids into downtown San Francisco for an evening excursion. We rode the trolleys, played Frisbee in the park, ate at a diner, then headed up to the top of Nob Hill to look over the city. It was a summer evening and the kids were full of electricity, chasing one another around trees and fountains in a little park at the top of the hill. One block away from the park sat Grace Cathedral. I asked the kids to follow me to the church. They followed in a wild mob, running and laughing before finally reaching the steps of the cathedral. Once we arrived I quieted them down and asked them to enter the church, find a place to sit, and spend 20 minutes reflecting on the day in prayer. The kids immediately protested, begging me to shorten the prayer time so they could get back to the running and screaming and flirting. I yielded and cut the time to 10 minutes. They thanked me profusely and then entered the cathedral.

I'd been inside the cathedral many times and was nervous that the kids would be disturbing to other people. But as soon as we entered the cavern-ous quiet and beauty of the cathedral, the kids fell silent. One by one they walked around soaking in the sacred art, the smell of incense, the candles that had been lit for prayer. Ten minutes later I walked to the back of the church and waited for the youth to join me. No one came. It would be another 15 min-utes before anyone joined me and 30 minutes be-fore the group was ready to leave. When I told the kids they'd had spent 40 minutes in prayer, most of them were surprised. "It felt like we entered into God's house," one young man reflected, "and there are no clocks in God's house."

Of course we don't all have a gorgeous cathedral we can take kids to, but there are other ways we can use space to help slow kids down for prayer. A candle in a darkened room often stops kids. So does sacred art and natural beauty. Most youth rooms are kid friendly with comfy couches, hip posters, and recreational furniture like pool and foosball tables. What if we made space that was also friendly to the souls of kids—rooms that youth found to be sacred, rooms that drew out their spiritual yearnings? Here are some thoughts to consider as you seek to create sacred space for the young people in your ministry.

Find Sacred Space

Where are the spaces within and around your church and community that are conducive to prayer? Where are the spaces that invite reflection or resonate with God's beauty and mystery? Try taking kids to these spaces to pray. What places work? What places seem distracting? Where do you think Jesus would withdraw to pray if he lived in your community? Where would you pray when you were an adolescent? Take the time to scout through cathedrals and churches, mountainsides and meadows in your area to find the places that invite prayer.

Create Sacred Space

Create a prayer space within your church. This might be a separate room or a corner of a room. Make it simple and beautiful. A cross, some candles, a bowl of water, some pillows, an empty bench. Keep it simple. Draw on what helps you to pray. Try not to overstimulate or manipulate with lots of spiritual kitsch. You don't need to entertain people to God or cover up the loneliness, quiet, or emptiness of prayer. Create a space that draws youth inward and outward—inward to the temple of their hearts and outward to the heart of the world.

Sometimes the spaces most conducive to helping youth pray are the spaces created by and with them. Invite the kids in your church to create a prayer space. You might begin by looking into the kinds of spaces they find helpful for prayer. Take them to places similar to the ones where Jesus prayed (mountaintops, wilderness, gardens). Find other places in town where people like to pray. Then together design and create a youth room or space that invites prayer.

—❧—

In the past few years I've noticed a trend within youth ministries and Christian conferences to create prayer spaces saturated and even cluttered with sacred objects. In a reflection of our consumer culture, prayer rooms are packed with candles, various crosses, bowls of water, ribbons, sacred pictures, ointments, pillows, kneeling pads, scent machines, prayer beads, bubble machines, videos of looping nature images, and on and on. It can be fun to create and experiment with various prayer "props," but I've found it most helpful if the prayer space is as simple and as spacious as possible. Otherwise we risk communicating that prayer is an exotic, otherworldly endeavor that requires all kinds of accoutrements.

I recently attended a youth conference on the East Coast that had a designated prayer room. Two artistic youth workers had spent hours creating a Disney-esque fantasy room full of religious paintings, candles, track lighting, streaming video from various cathedrals, crosses of every shape and size, Gregorian chant music, and much more. The prayer room really gave you the sense of stepping into another world. I watched kids become mesmerized by the bubble machine, the candles, the video images, the artificial scents, the electric waterfalls, and the dimly lit icons. To many it looked like the kids were praying (and maybe some of them were). They certainly were quiet and enraptured, but were they praying? I'm not so sure. My observation was that the youth seemed so overwhelmed and distracted by the creativity and power of the various gadgets that they became passive observers, rather than engaged participants. Many of them were so excited by everything that they kept moving from one cool sacred object to another, like children in a toy store.

On the last night of the conference, a youth worker asked me my thoughts on the prayer room. I told him I thought it was a very creative expression but, in my experience, not the kind of room that invited prayer. The youth worker looked relieved, and then told me he'd taken his youth group into the prayer room the previous night, but felt his kids were mostly distracted by all the images and candles. Eventually, he had them leave and go across the hall to an empty conference room. They cleared out chairs, made a circle in the middle of the floor, dimmed the lights, and brought over a single candle from the prayer room. "It was one of the best nights of prayer we've had…"

The focus of prayer is on God. The real question is: What kind of environment helps us to bring our true selves to the true God?

6 Embody

He continued to go to his house, which had windows in its upper room open towards Jerusalem, and to get down on his knees three times a day to pray to his God.
—DANIEL 6:10

Human beings generally find their physical bodies to be a confusing mix of ecstasy, desire, temptation, and shame. While our bodies can be a source of tremendous joy, there may be no other aspect of our humanity that brings out such strong feelings of guilt, disappointment, discomfort, and self-hatred. According to the National Eating Disorders Association, 80 percent of American women and 45 percent of American men are dissatisfied with their bodies. If my experience leading prayer workshops is any indication, many readers will skip this chapter simply because of the resistance and uncomfortable feelings that often arise when we are asked to become aware of our physical selves.

Yet in the Christian faith, the body remains deeply necessary to our spiritual liberation—despite our attempts to separate it, disregard it, indulge it, starve it, and beat it with various spiritual ascetics. The Christian life not only includes but depends upon our bodies. Our bodies are the means through which we give and receive love with others, and it is through our bodies that we experience and know God. It is Jesus' incarnation of the Divine that blesses the human body. Yet we find it hard to receive this blessing when Jesus' own life, as recorded in the Scriptures, shines little insight on how to deal with the sexual pressures, eating disorders, and body image obsessions that are part of daily life in Western society.

From the gospel accounts we can glean that Jesus wants us to live with bodies open and receptive to all of life's pain and beauty. Jesus heals eyes, ears, limbs, and hearts so we might see, hear, feel, and know the truth of God's presence among us. Jesus' willingness to embrace children, touch lepers, and receive touch from outcasts communicates his love for the human body.

In the praying tradition we find many different ways in which Christians have employed their bodies as companions in prayer. Kneeling, laying prostrate, fasting...in fact, the primary objective of many prayer methods is to help human beings integrate mind, spirit, and body in prayer.

How do we help young people know God with their bodies? How can young people experience their bodies as mediators, bearers, and instruments of the Holy? Maybe the clearest experiences we can give young people of God's love and grace are those in which young people feel accepted and at peace within their own skin.

Stretch Out

One of the most important elements in inviting youth into prayer is giving them the space to get comfortable with God. There is a heightened sense of self-consciousness during adolescence. Young people worry about how they smell, look, and sound to other young people. This self-consciousness can prevent kids from relaxing in prayer. One way to ease this anxiety is to give kids plenty of space to pray. I like to have kids pray in large open spaces (like outdoors or the sanctuary of a church where they can lie down on pews). This allows them to move, get comfortable, and avoid the temptation of elbowing, pushing, tickling, or flirting with nearby friends. Sometimes just giving kids wide-open space to pray better communicates the spaciousness and openness of God than the particular method of prayer we employ.

Body Postures

The way kids arrange their bodies can sometimes affect their prayers. Classic prayer positions include kneeling, lying down, sitting (with the spine straight), standing (sometimes with head raised), and pacing slowly (as many monks do within their cells). I've found that when I ask kids to find a place to pray and take a position that will help them pray, they often (perhaps intuitively) choose one of these classical prayer positions. Other times I tell kids about these various classical positions and how keeping our spines straight and our lungs open may help our bodies be more open and attentive in prayer.

Here is one simple exercise I've often used with young people: After the youth all find places in the room to pray, I invite them to close their eyes and place their hands on their laps with their fingers curled in (like a fist). I invite them to spend a few moments noticing what it's like to be in the presence of God and others with their hands closed. After a few minutes of silence I invite them to slowly roll out their fingers until their hands are open. I then ask them to spend a few minutes noticing what it's like to be in the presence of God with their hands open. After three to five minutes I gently draw the attention of the group back to the front of the room and ask them to share their experiences.

Breathe

In silent prayer exercises I often invite kids to notice their breathing. There's something about paying attention to this most basic, life-sustaining function that helps quiet the mind and open the heart for prayer. I'm careful to remind kids not to alter or change their breathing pattern, but to simply notice each in-breath and out-breath with a sense of gratitude. Sometimes I invite them to count each breath, without altering or changing their breathing pattern, just noticing their breathing as a gift from God.

See

Placing a candle, a cross, or another sacred visual image as a focal point for prayer can help kids quiet and prepare themselves for prayer. I often light a candle and remind the youth that the light from the candle is a symbol of the light of Christ in the world. While some people close their eyes in prayer, others find praying with closed eyes to be awkward. A candle or other visual symbol can help youth find a resting place for their eyes while their hearts turn to God.

Hear

Music is the language of the heart, and the heart is where God's love resides. One of the best ways to encourage prayer within young people is to find sacred music that opens their hearts, minds, bodies, and spirits to God. Many youth groups rely on popular praise music for worship and youth activities. When inviting kids to pray, I like to find sacred music that is intended as prayer. I play sacred music at the beginning of prayer times as a way of helping kids enter into prayer. It's also nice to play sacred music at bedtime when we're on retreat. Music like the prayer chants from the community at Taizé works on a different level than Christian pop music. Many students find that such music draws their souls to God. Just listening to the music can become an experience of prayer.

Touch

A Franciscan priest led a unique prayer experience at one conference I attended. In the room set aside for prayer, he placed various textures on the floor, on tables, and on walls. As people came to the entrance to pray, the priest would blindfold them, and individual guides would lead people into the room and around to various objects, inviting them to pray through their sense of touch. They might come to a bowl of sand and pray while the sand ran through their fingers, or sit and be wrapped in a heavy blanket of velvet, or hold warm stones in their hands. When people wanted to move on, they would simply signal their accompanier in silence, who would then guide them to the next object. The power in this experience was not only in praying through touch and physical sensation, but also in feeling the guiding hand of seeing companions, guiding you from one prayer to the next.

—◦◦◦—

The first blessings we receive in this world come through our bodies. As babies we are held, kissed, and snuggled. We see caring faces and hear cooing voices. These physical sensations are love's first communication. Over time each of us will receive other messages as well—the shout of abusive anger, the sight of shaming disapproval, the sting of a slapped face—and these too are messages that will form our sense of self, God, and other. It's not only our spirits, our emotions, our hearts and minds that seek God—it is our bodies as well. Our bodies also seek to be liberated from the shame and abuse they've suffered. Our bodies seek a blessing from God.

Can we welcome and heal the bodies of young people? Can we create ministries that invite young people to bring their bodies into prayer? Is it possible that the youth within your community might bring themselves, body and soul, before Jesus so that he might touch them, bless them, and whisper in their ears, "Ephphatha" (Be opened).

7 Keep Silence

> But the Lord is in his holy temple; let all the earth keep silence before him!
>
> —HABAKKUK 2:20

"Silence leads to prayer. Prayer leads to faith. Faith leads to service. Service leads to peace." In these wise words, Mother Teresa recognized that the Christian journey often begins in silence.[12] It is in silence that we come to terms with the reality of who we are, the reality of the world around us, and the reality of God.

Young people are being raised in a world terrified of silence. In our culture silence is often taken to mean that something is lacking, something is missing. We fear the dreaded loneliness that might overtake us if we were forced to live without the talking pictures, the jingly pop songs, and

---

[12] *Come Be My Light* (Doubleday, 2007).

the life-absorbing amusements that fill up all our unscheduled moments. Silence is likened to going without—to be lacking and poor. Keeping silence insinuates you are on the outside of the whirring culture with its chatty celebrities, pulsing beats, and attention-grabbing diversions. We fear silence in Western culture because it means the death of consumer culture—televisions turned off, computers shut down, cell phones gone dead, musical devices unplugged. Who would we be and what kind of life would we possess without our electronic devices? In silence there is only the stark struggle to perceive life as it really is.

Young people are often even more suspicious of silence than adults are. Not only have young people absorbed the consumer culture's fear of silence, the official silences they do encounter are mostly imposed by agitated adults. For most young people the word *silence* evokes experiences of being "shushed" by teachers and parents who want young people to hold back, restrain their impulses, and focus their attention on the presenting adult. In this way silence becomes an experience of conformity, of withholding that which is fun, natural, noisy, and relational—in order to please an authority.

For young people, keeping silence might be seen as an experience of being exiled from the umbilical cord of movie previews, pop gossip, music downloads, news blogs, television episodes, commercial flashes, chat rooms, and gaming sites on which American culture subsists. Over time most young people lose their ability to perceive in silence the convicting wonder and reflection from childhood. Silence becomes a dead thing, every disconnection from the sounds and relationships around them a cause for loneliness, emptiness, and self-pity.

The work in ministering with young people is to recover and redeem silence. Not the shameful, shunning silence, but the silence from which God created and sustained the world. Silence is food for the soul. Silence is how we learn to listen and discern the voice of God. Silence is how we hear suffering. Silence is how we learn to befriend others. Silence, as Mother Teresa stated, is not only the beginning of prayer, it is the way to peace.

For a young person the silences that give rise to prayer are often stolen from a culture that seeks to occupy every moment. In my conversations with young people, I've discovered the silences of faith are often found at the margins of their lives—in those unscheduled, unexpected moments when the demands of school, parents, and culture unexpectedly let up. It is the silence that descends on a young woman while she lies in the dark of her bedroom; the silence that accompanies an adolescent boy as he walks through an empty neighborhood; the silence that blankets a 17-year-old girl as she rides the city bus; the silence that surrounds a 13-year-old boy as he waits, groggy-eyed, for the Sunday service to begin. It is the silence a high school senior feels as he looks at a flood-damaged apartment building in New Orleans or the quiet that comes over a talkative middle school girl as she stares into a campfire with a makeshift community of friends.

It turns out that it is often in these discarded, unnoticed silences that young people spontaneously feel and receive the presence of God.[13] How can our ministries with youth encourage these moments of silent reflection? How do we give permission for kids to sit back, withdraw from the chatter of their friends, and sit, like Mary, at Jesus' feet, listening and attentive?

One of my touchstones in youth ministry is *The Chosen* by Chaim Potok, a book about the struggle of two Jewish fathers to impart faith to their sons. Danny, the central character of the book, is being raised to take his father's place as a Tzaddik, the rabbinical leader of a Hassidic community. His father

---

[13] This is not only true in my own interviews with young people but was first noticed in a study of junior high students by David and Sally Elkind. See "Varieties of Religious Experience in Young Adolescents," *Journal for the Scientific Study of Religion 2* (Fall 1962): 102-12. I first became aware of the large amount of time that adolescents spend alone (up to 25 percent of their time) in the work of Mihály Csíkszentmihályi and Reed Larson in *Being Adolescent: Conflict and Growth in the Teenage Years* (New York: Basic Books, 1984).

stopped speaking to Danny when he was 10, raising him in silence to help his son apprehend his own soul and the reality of God within a suffering world. Toward the end of the book 17-year-old Danny tells his friend Reuven what he's learned from spending much of his adolescence in silence:

"You can listen to silence, Reuven. I've begun to realize that you can listen to silence and learn from it. It has a quality and a dimension all its own. It talks to me sometimes. I feel myself alive in it. It talks. And I can hear it."

The words came out in a soft singsong. He sounded exactly like his father.

"You don't understand that, do you?" he asked.

"No."

He nodded. "I didn't think you would."

"What do you mean, it talks to you?"

"You have to want to listen to it, and then you can hear it. It has a strange, beautiful texture. It doesn't always talk. Sometimes—sometimes it cries, and you can hear the pain of the world in it. It hurts to listen to it then. But you have to."[14]

[14] Fawcett Crest, 1967, 249.

How do we begin to invite youth into the living silence of God? How do we help them befriend silence as a place from which our prayer is empowered? How do we help them hear not only the "strange, beautiful texture" of silence, but Jesus' cry to carry and respond to the pain of the world?

Notice God

One way we can encourage young people to experience silence as prayer is by helping them notice the silences that are already present in their lives. Silence can seem so awkward and strange to students at first, so I try to help them see that they are actually quite familiar with silence. I ask them to tell me all the times in the day when they are quiet. Often kids will give me moments like listening to music, reading a book, riding a bus, sitting in their backyard, cruising the Internet, lying in bed at night, walking outside, or skateboarding through the park. I ask them to tell me what these different silences are like. Then I show them the many places in Scripture where Jesus went up to a mountain or off to a lakeside or deserted place for prayer and quiet. I ask if they've ever had moments when they've gone someplace by themselves to get away from everyone and just think or pray or reflect on their lives. Most kids can recall experiences like this. I help them see that Jesus often felt that silence and solitude helped him pray.

My hope in this conversation is that kids will see silence as something ordinary and familiar, not strange and otherworldly. Not only is this helpful for the moments of silent prayer these kids will experience in my ministry, it also invites them to experience the various silences in their lives as times ripe with prayer, times that Jesus experienced as susceptible to the presence of God.

Sometimes I'll give kids an assignment. I ask them to look and listen for God the next time they're in silence—the way they might listen to a good friend sitting next to them. I invite them to simply "glance" at God with the eyes of their heart, seeking to notice the presence of God within the quiet spaces of their lives.

When we gather again I ask kids to share what it was like to listen for God within the silences of their week. Sometimes they share important moments of prayer and awareness, but often they tell me they forgot the assignment. From time to time I give the little assignment again, asking kids to look and listen for God within the quiet and unscheduled moments of their day. Over time, my hope is that the students in my group will be more watchful and receptive to God, and less resistant to the quiet places within their lives.

Little Sips of Silence

In Sunday school classes, youth meetings, and other programmed times with kids, I try to provide what one friend of mine calls "little sips of silence." When I give an opening or closing prayer, I pause between the words so kids can feel their own prayers within them. If we're on retreat or at a summer camp or service project, I will have kids stop their conversations to look around and quietly take in their surroundings. If we're having a Bible study or class discussion and someone says something poignant, I'll ask the group to stop the conversation for a minute or two and let the words or insight sink in. If we're driving to an event or camp, I'll have sections of our trip where I'll ask kids to cease conversations and just take in the scenery around them. These little sips of silence aren't official "prayer exercises." They are just little pauses—little spaces that give room for the soul of a young person to breathe. They are an attempt to create a ministry culture that is spacious and porous to God's Spirit.

The Quakers often practice this kind of spontaneous silence. Within a Quaker business meeting, work outing, or project, a community member can "call for silence." The group responds by ceasing their work and conversations for a few moments in order to become more aware of the Holy Spirit's presence among them. Little sips of silence can help a ministry become more attentive to and aware of the Spirit of God.

Befriend Distractions

Of course, it's also important to give young people periods of silence that are more directly intended for prayer. Many of the prayer methods presented in this book take place in silence. Yet even when you have a beautifully lit room with candles and contemplative music, silent prayer can sometimes be extremely uncomfortable (for adults and youth)—especially if you are not familiar with the inevitable distractions that arise in silence. When engaging students in any sort of silent prayer, it's important to let them know that everyone who prays experiences distracting thoughts and feelings from time to time. Teresa of Avila, one of the great teachers of prayer within the Christian tradition, once said that every time she quieted for prayer she'd immediately become aware of a thousand thoughts and feelings—as if a wild herd of horses were set loose bucking and neighing through her brain. As soon as we enter into silence we often become aware of all kinds of things. Sometimes I give kids an example of the kind of thing that can happen when we sit down to pray in silence:

As soon as I close my eyes I notice an itchy spot on my back and wonder if it's a pimple, which makes me think about swimming at the YMCA, because they have a chlorinated pool that dries up my skin causing less oily buildup on my back, which makes me think of the Friday night basketball game at the YMCA and how I need to show up early so I get on a good team, which reminds me I need to practice if I want to make the varsity team this year, which sends me into a daydream about Sarah Miles coming to the games and watching me play, which suddenly makes me anxious because it's possible I might sit the bench, which gives me second thoughts about going out for the basketball team, which causes me to fantasize about sitting next to Sarah Miles at a basketball game while my friends are playing, which suddenly makes me nervously happy at the thought of being next to Sarah, which turns to a tightening fear when I think of trying to talk to her, but then it occurs to me I could text message her, which makes me frustrated that I've already

hit my text messaging limit for this month, which
makes me angry at my parents for getting such
a stupid cell phone plan with such limited text
messaging capabilities…

Again, it's important to let kids know that everyone encounters these kinds of thought streams and distractions when seeking to pray and attend to God in silence. I then tell students that all we can do in silence is seek to be with God. It is our desire to pray and be with God that is most pleasing to God. When they notice their minds wandering in prayer, I encourage them to turn their attention back to God and say something to the effect of, "I want to be with you," or as my friend Brennan Manning says, "I belong to you." Any simple phrase or image will do, as long as it draws attention back to God. We turn to God in silent prayer, our mind wanders, we return to our prayer, our mind wanders, we return to our prayer. It's important that young people realize this is the work of prayer—seeking to be present to the One who loves them, even when their minds are busy and distracted by the sound of ten thousand neighing horses.

Live in Silence

For years I've helped lead camps and retreats in which young people spend extended mornings or full days in silence. This past summer I helped lead a national gathering of Presbyterian youth in which five thousand youth and their adult leaders all spent a whole morning in silence. I've found young people to be incredibly receptive and grateful for these radical invitations to turn their attention from their friends and activities and seek communion with God. Many of them appreciate these extended periods of silence as a welcome respite from the pressure, speed, and noise of the culture. I often feel that, for youth, moments of extended silence are invitations to move from talking about faith to actually experiencing faith firsthand.

There are a few important things to remember when inviting kids into extended times of silence. First, make them aware of the distractions they'll likely encounter (see the exercise above). Second, suggest different ways in which they might seek God's presence within the silence. I invite kids to use the time as if they're spending the day with an old friend they haven't seen for a while. I tell them to rest, enjoy the outdoors, pray, read, journal, draw, and allow themselves to simply enjoy and be grateful for the life God has given them. Third, I think it's important to start any extended time of silence with a time of prayer in which we offer the time to God, asking Jesus for a deepening sense of his presence and companionship. There needs to be some way of helping kids center and marking the time as set apart for prayer and reflection. I also like to close any extended silence with a prayer in which we offer thanks to God for whatever we've become aware of in the silence.

I also think it's important to gather students together after these times of extended silence and give them space and time to talk about their experiences. This offers young people a chance to name (and in that way "capture") their experience of God within the quiet. It also gives kids a chance to hear the diverse ways in which other young people experience God, and the leadership a chance to gain insight into the spiritual experiences and struggles of the young people within the ministry.

—✺—

Now there was a great wind, so strong that it was splitting mountains and breaking rocks in pieces before the Lord, but the Lord was not in the wind; and after the wind an earthquake, but the Lord was not in the earthquake; and after the earthquake a fire, but the Lord was not in the fire; and after the fire a sound of sheer silence…then there came a voice to him that said, "What are you doing here, Elijah?"

—1 KINGS 19:11-13

God speaks to Elijah not through the overwhelming spectacles of wind, earthquake, and fire, but through a "sheer silence." Teenagers live within a culture enamored by power and pomp, a culture that has lost its ability to hear the quiet sacrifices, the hidden creativity, and the humble acts of love that continue to sustain our world. Our young people need the silence of God so that they too might hear God say to them, "Who are you? What are you doing here? What is it you desire in this life?"

8 Read

In the beginning was the Word, and the Word was with God, and the Word was God.

—JOHN 1:1

On my fifth birthday my paternal grandparents ("Boppa" and "Nonie") presented me with my first real book. It was a thick, brown, cloth-covered, wizard's tome of a book, embossed with gold cursive lettering that read, "The Bible." In the center of the hardback cover was a sepia colored, wallet-sized headshot of Jesus, posing stoically like a Civil War soldier.

What I remember most is the book's weight, which seemed to signify a kind of import, like I was being handed the collected wisdom of my elders. Unable to open and balance the heavy gift in my five-year-old hands, my grandparents led me to their couch, spread the volume open on my lap, and then left me to explore. Flipping through the glossy gold-edged pages I found chapter after chapter of indecipherable words, separated here and there by realistic drawings of ancient people wearing turbans, animal skins, floor-length robes, and strange tunics. These were not the friendly cartoon images of my children's storybooks. These images exposed the hidden passions of adult life: a mob of half-naked men goring one another with spears while a white-bearded man lifted his arms to the sky; a bare-backed woman disrobing near a pool of water while a king with a gold pointed crown watched in secret; a young woman kneeling with a basin before a seated Jesus, her face tilted in devotion and her black hair draped softly across his naked feet; a boy thrashing in the dirt, white spittle oozing from his mouth, his helpless father pleading shamelessly toward the unshakable face of Jesus. Toward the final pages was a coal-darkened image of a group of men huddled in a windowless room watching cautiously as one man pressed his thumb into the rough, red scars of Jesus' open, unflinching hands.

As evocative as these pictures were, none of them held my attention as much as the image I discovered on the inside of the back cover. It was a realistic painting of the swirling blue earth. Its upper right side was shrouded in night, with speckled stars and a glowing gray moon, while the lower left shimmered in emerald blues, lit up by the burning yellow sun. With my finger I traced the earth with its puzzle-plots of land and cloud-patched ocean. I felt my head break open at the thought that I was holding the world, and the world was holding me, and all of it—earth and sun and night and oceans, ancient stories and the mysteries of the world that lay behind and in front of me—all of this was somehow enfolded by this mysterious, ancient, present God.

This book sat at my bedside throughout my childhood. From time to time I would place it on my pillow and flip through its pages, staring ponderously at the passionate, uncensored world of these hardheaded human beings and their struggles to be good. Eventually, I would learn to read the stories themselves— which had been cleansed of numbered verses, then paraphrased and written out like tales told on a hunting trip. I found the stories shockingly riveting—filled with blood, betrayal, erotic passion, desperation, greed, yearning, cruelty, loyalty, dreams, omens, miraculous healings, heartbreak, wisdom, and self-sacrificing acts of love.

Reading and rereading that mysterious book, I somehow sensed why Gregory the Great (sixth century) called the Bible a "letter from God" that disclosed "God's heart in God's words." This book, the only book I owned until fifth grade, revealed the world within the world. It pointed to a third dimension, a spiritual realm that worked within, beneath, and beyond the surface of things. This book gave me a lens that caused me to see and feel differently about my life. I began to look for signs. I began to sense that my life carried the same significance and drama as the lives of these ancient people who knew God at the beginning. Like them I had a choice to follow and listen for the wisdom and guidance of God or to stubbornly pursue my own happiness and security. I expected that God would someday visit me with dreams and signs, prophecies and late-night whispers. I began to pray and wait and trust, seeking to imitate the Bible's faithful and avoid the mistakes of its foolish, trusting that one day this same God would speak a word to me.

I don't know how others come to know the Bible. I suspect that few young people today carry the same feelings of awe and wonder and gratitude and mystery that I was lucky enough to experience. It saddens me that most of the youth I've known and worked with experience the Bible as simply one among an Amazon of books, one set of stories amid a satellite dish of stories, one set of images amid a broadband of images.

But I have discovered that teaching kids to pray with the Bible opens the possibility of their recovering the Bible as sacred text. To do that we must help young people encounter the Bible as a holy rendezvous, a temple, a place of prayer. We have to help them experience Scripture not only as a source of religious information and instruction, but more importantly as a book that contains within its pages the possibility of hearing from God directly.

By teaching young people to pray the Bible, we invite them to enter the words of Scripture with anticipation. We encourage young people to come to the words and images of Scripture just as people came to Jesus—carrying their pain, their need, their curiosity, their desire to live more fully. To invite young people to pray with the Bible is to help them come to Scripture in search of not just the teachings of Jesus, but the love and companionship of Jesus himself.

There are many ways in which Christians come to Scripture with a sense of prayer and vulnerability to God. Here are two ways I've found to be most helpful in teaching young people to approach the Bible with prayerful expectation:

Sacred Reading

In sacred reading, otherwise known by the Latin words *lectio divina*, we're invited to hear the Bible as if each word is pregnant with revelation. Sacred reading is an ancient method of praying the words of Scripture, one that stretches back to the beginning of monastic life and even further into the religious practice of our Jewish sisters and brothers.[15] It is the practice of opening ourselves to the presence of God through reading and meditating on the Word of God. Although it begins with reading the words of Scripture, the experience of *lectio divina* is more analogous to talking with a dear friend than to reading a newspaper. In *lectio*, as in any intimate relationship, it is not the words we attend to as much as the person who is speaking.

When inviting young people to practice *lectio divina*, it's helpful to begin by explaining that Christians see the Bible as the revelation of God. We hold the words of the Bible as sacred words—words that can heal us, convict us, change us, and carry us into a closer relationship with the living God. When we pray the Bible, we listen to the words of Scripture as a love letter from God. We read a short passage two or three times, listening for a particular word that seems to stand out for us, address us, disturb us, or comfort us. We receive this word as if God were picking it up and handing it to us. We then take this word and hold

[15] See Basil Pennington, *Lectio Divina* (Crossroad, 1998), ix.

it within the deepest recesses of our heart. We repeat this word over and over, noticing the feelings and thoughts that come to us as we repeat this word gently within. We then allow ourselves to pray, to speak to God whatever words or feelings we have within us, all that has been stirred up by this word from Scripture. We pray to God until we are spent. Finally, we allow ourselves to rest. We rest in gratitude for the word, for the insight, but most of all for God's presence to us.

Here are the steps I follow when leading *lectio divina* with young people:

Preparation. After setting up the room for prayer (dimming lights, lighting candles), I explain the steps of the prayer and describe the Scripture we'll be praying over, giving them any background on the passage that might help them in the prayer. (I've found that this prayer can be most helpful after Bible study when students have had time to really discuss and study a particular passage.) I talk about the prayer as seeking to be with God through the words of the Bible. I tell them how long the silence will last and give them some suggestions for handling distractions. I invite the young people to find a place in the room where they can pray. I may remind them of classical praying positions such as sitting with back straight, lying down, or gently pacing.

Silence. After everyone seems comfortable, I lead the group in a simple, prayerful song, chant, or some sort of centering exercise to help them focus their attention on God. I might say something like, "Take a moment to rest, relaxing into God's presence. With each breath become aware of God's love for you. When you're ready, say a simple prayer offering yourself to God and welcoming whatever the Holy Spirit seeks to bring you in the prayer." I allow a few moments of silence.

Reading. I invite the young people to listen for a word or phrase that seems to address them. I remind them not to force anything, but to simply listen for a word that seems to stand out, like it's in bold or italics. I then read the biblical passage three times. I try to choose a short passage, often an encounter with Jesus or some other passage that relates to the particular theme we're working on. The first reading is at a fairly normal pace. I deliberately read more slowly during the second and third readings. Sometimes I ask a different person to do each reading; different voices emphasize different words and allow the Scripture to be heard with fresh ears.

Meditation. After the third reading I invite the youth to prayerfully repeat the word within themselves, allowing the rest of the passage to fall away.

I remind kids to notice what thoughts, feelings, and images come to them as they pray the word. "What do you notice about this word? What is being offered?"

Prayer. After five minutes or so I invite the youth to express themselves to Jesus. Sometimes I'll give them paper and pencil and let them write out whatever feelings or thoughts have come to them. Other times I'll invite them to pray whatever feelings, desires, requests, or gratitudes have come to them in the prayer. I ask them to speak their honest thoughts and feelings to Jesus or the Holy Spirit until there is nothing left to share.

Rest. After a few minutes I invite the young people simply to rest in God, the way a child, spent from crying, might finally rest upon his mother's lap. I invite the youth to allow God to hold all their thoughts and feelings, all their worries and cares, and simply rest within the One who loves them.

Testimony. After a few minutes of quiet I gently gather the group together and invite them to share what took place in their prayer. Sometimes I'll give them time to journal before gathering them together. I try to allow as many students to speak as possible. I also ask how many kids fell asleep or didn't have a word strike them during the prayer. Usually a few hands will go up. I reassure them that this kind of experience happens to everyone, even veteran praying Christians, and it simply means we're tired or maybe this isn't the best way for us to pray at this time.

Let me give an example of how one young person experienced this prayer during an exercise I did just a few weeks ago with a group of teens. After helping the group get settled, I read Mark 4:35-41 in which Jesus stills a storm. At the close of the prayer I asked the young people to share their experiences. A shaggy-haired boy of 14 shared the following (my paraphrase):

> The word that first came to me was "cushion." Jesus was sleeping on a cushion. I thought, "That's weird! Where did Jesus get a cushion?" I didn't really think this was the right kind of word to pray about so I just let it go, but the second time you read the passage, there it was again, "cushion." It just stuck in my brain. So I thought, "Okay, God, I guess I'll pray 'cushion.'" So I started praying this word over and over—"cushion," "cushion," "cushion." I was just saying it slowly for the longest time. Then I noticed I was starting to feel really sad—like this really heavy sadness was pressing

on my chest. I didn't know what was going on, but I just kept praying, "cushion." And then suddenly I started to remember my grandmother, lying on this red velvet pillow on her couch when she was sick and dying. And I remember my mom and everyone was at her house. And I remember everyone was really irritated and there was all this bickering going on between my mom and her siblings about whether to get grandmother to a hospice or not. Just a bunch of arguments. I was only 10 years old, and I remember just feeling really sad and really unsure of what was happening. And I remember looking at my grandmother, and she wasn't listening to any of the arguing. She was just looking at me and smiling. And I remembered that I just stood there smiling back, and I wanted to go over and hug her, but instead I just stood with my parents and stared at my grandmother and smiled at her. So I just thought about that moment in the prayer. And I prayed for my grandmother. And I prayed for my mom who still misses her. And I started crying a little because I wish I had just gone over and hugged her. And I felt like God was smiling at me like my grandmother and telling me to be like her and not get caught up in all the worries about school and other stuff that doesn't matter. And after that I just felt incredibly peaceful and just lay on the ground until I think I might've fallen asleep.

Praying the Psalms

There is a wellspring of life within the Psalms. The Psalms express all the gratitude, anguish, hope, suffering, lust, jealousy, joy, peacefulness, vindictiveness, grief, grace, contentment, fear, love, hatred, and compassion that human beings carry within their hearts. Over the centuries Christians have turned to the Psalms to express their prayers. One exercise I've found particularly helpful is to make copies of a variety of psalms. (Sometimes it's nice to find a more evocative, poetic translation, such as Eugene Peterson's *The Message*.) I give a little history on the Psalms as the prayers of the Jewish people, prayers that Jesus himself often prayed. Then I hand out the various psalms to the youth, and ask them to spend a few moments reading the psalms and identifying the various emotions that are being expressed. I tell students to write words like "very, very sad," "grief," "super bitter," or "fighting angry," every time they notice a particular emotion being expressed. I remind them that there may be many different emotions expressed in one psalm.

After five minutes or so I take out a whiteboard or flipchart and ask the kids to tell me all the different emotions they heard in the various psalms. I write these on the board. Often we create a list of 30 to 40 different emotions that range from "violent hatred" to "hot love" to "really sad" to "peaceful" to "super happy." I then ask the youth to take some time to go and actually pray the psalm that was given to them—pray the psalm to God as if it were their own words. I tell them to pay attention and see if certain lines or words really express something they might be feeling at this time. After a few minutes we gather again and talk about what happened. I'll ask them to share any words or sentences that really spoke to them. I write these on the board. I then hand out blank paper and ask the youth to go out and ask God to help them write their own psalms, with each student writing a psalm that expresses his or her heart's prayer at this time. After 15 minutes or so, I gather the group together and invite them to read the prayers.

I've noticed that this exercise can give kids a broader experience of the life of prayer. They see that prayer doesn't have to be "holy" and "pristine," but can contain all the mess and frustration and desperation of human life. Sometimes I'll collect the psalms the young people have written and post them in the youth room or give them to our worship committee to be incorporated into our worship services.

—⟨⟨⟩⟩—

To pray the Bible is to become intimate, not only with the words of Scripture, but also with the God from whom the words of Scripture emerge. Praying Scripture invites the young person to experience the Bible as an oasis of spirit, a place where the hidden life of love is unveiled, redeeming and reshaping a young person's world. Over time the Bible becomes not just another textbook, but a companion, a locket that contains the true image of the world, a resting place where young people can return—no matter how far they've traveled—and be carried home to the truth that waits beyond all understanding.

9 Go Outside

Praise him, sun and moon;

praise him, all you shining stars!

Praise him, you highest heavens,

and you waters above the heavens!

—PSALM 148:3-4

Although I couldn't hear her or see her face, I could tell Julia was crying. It was the way she brought her hands to her cheeks—first the left, then the right. The way she bowed her head, gently pressing her eyes against outstretched fingers. Sitting a short distance behind her I became anxious. Why was she crying? What was going on that I didn't know about? I watched, wanting to be sure. Then she turned, her profile exposed. I looked carefully at her eyes—they were glistening, swollen with tears.

I stood and looked up and down the Oregon coastline. Twenty high school students and five parent chaperones sat evenly spaced across the salt-and-pepper sand, their rose-tinted faces turned toward the setting sun. I followed their gaze. The horizon was wrapped in a warm blanket of lavender. The sun, tender and soft, was veiled in newborn pinks and reds. Beneath the skyline the ocean rocked back and forth, sending hushed swells across the sand as calming as a lullaby.

It was July, and I had tricked, cajoled, and bribed most of the high school kids at St. Andrew's Presbyterian Church to spend a weekend on the Oregon coast. Dispensing with the subtleties of Christian formation, I'd decided to get down to basics. The theme of the retreat was simply "God." What were our honest experiences of God? What were our beliefs about God? And how did this compare with the God that Jesus knew and proclaimed?

I was in my fourth year as director of youth ministry at St. Andrew's and felt like a veteran when it came to weekend youth events. After three years of trial and error, I'd found the right combination of fun, food, fellowship, and faith that caused even the most Buddahgnostic of teenagers to sing, "Lord, I lift your name on high!" by the last night's campfire meeting.

But here we were on the first night of the retreat, and I'd already discarded my soul-winning schedule. We played Frisbee and built sand castles. We soaked in sunbeams and waded in the waves. The normal posing and posturing that was so common among this group of high schoolers had disappeared. They were kids again, freed by the surf and sun. The play was contagious. Even the most sterile of parents had wrenched off shoes and stockings, rolled up pant legs, grabbed hands with hollering teenagers, and played jump rope with the tumbling seashore.

Soon the sun began to descend and it was time for our evening "lesson time." Noticing how we all felt alive and enchanted by the ocean and sand, I decided to take a risk and disregard my planned program. I called the group together and told them that in place of the evening meeting I wanted people to simply sit by themselves in silence and prayer and watch the sun set. I said a small prayer to bless our time, then sent them out across the sand.

After everyone settled, I strolled nonchalantly behind the students. Every few steps or so I paused and turned my eyes toward the sun. When I was sure no one was watching, I looked carefully at the backs of students, and was startled to see signs of distress. Julia wasn't the only one who seemed upset. A shirtsleeve dragged across the eyes. Hands carefully wiping each cheek. Had there been a rift between friends? A break-up within one of our youth group romances? Who was involved and how had I missed it?

My pastoral alarm told me it was time to intervene. Putting on my counselor face I sauntered up to Katie, a 15-year-old girl whose eyelashes, I now could see, were heavy with tears. "Hey, Katie," I spoke gently. "How are you?" Looking down she gave me the standard response: "Good." I went straight to the point, "Katie, I've noticed that you and Julia are both crying. You want to tell me what's going on?" She looked at me open and straightforward. "I've never seen a sunset before. It's so amazing. I just started crying."

I was thrown off balance and embarrassed that I'd missed the obvious. I'd been so busy playing my role as "retreat leader," I'd missed what God was doing. Katie was right. It was beautiful—the emptying sky, the endless blue of the ocean, the chanting waves, and the sun's liturgical descent.

"I don't know why Julia's crying," she offered. "Maybe she's never seen a sunset, either."

Later that night, sitting by the fireplace drinking hot chocolate, we had perhaps the most honest discussion about life and faith that I've ever experienced with high school students. Something had shifted within the group. The kids were no longer squirrelly. The serenity of the beach was still with us. The difference between youth and adults had diminished. We listened carefully to one another wondering aloud about the mystery of life and God.

We are losing the intimacy that human beings once experienced with the created world. We are losing our ability to see, feel, taste, touch, and hear the natural world around us. Most of us in the developed world spend the majority of our time in artificial environments, insulated from the colors and textures of the world around us. We warm ourselves with the flick of a switch; we sleep and wake unmindful of the moon's rhythms; we pull fish from our freezers without smelling the salt of the sea, collect store-bought lettuce without getting dirt on our hands, and walk through homes and offices ignorant of the fragrance of the forests that made those structures possible. Author Janet Finch declares that we in affluent societies have become grievously "de-natured," living lives in which the five senses have been displaced. Finch writes,

> We know something is missing. And yet we flatter ourselves to believe that we are the advantaged souls, compared to those who walk in the out-of-

doors, who cook over the smoke of a wood fire, who make their own music, who dig in the dirt, who lift and carry, who sweat in the heat of the sun, and who in the cold wrap themselves in quilts and skins. People who grow or kill their own food or shop for it in bazaars full of completely unfiltered sounds and smells and sights. We consider them disadvantaged and ourselves rich. Yet who, in this most fundamental way, is starving? I was 20 years old before I saw the moonrise for myself.[16]

One of the things I love most about Jesus is that he wants us to become fully alive. The liberation he offers isn't limited to the mind; it seeks to touch eyes, ears, hands, and heart. It seeks to escort prisoners out from damp and dim cells into the bright sun of the day. I don't think it was a coincidence that Jesus spent much of his time teaching and ministering outside. For Jesus, God's presence was easily accessed in silent mountains, churning seas, lonely deserts, fragrant gardens, and the heat and dust of the open road. Jesus found signs of God's presence in fig trees and lilies, mustard seeds and ravens, stones and healing mud. Praying people have always sought places that

[16] Alan Cheuse and Lisa Alvarez, ed. "Coming to Your Senses," *Writers Workshop in a Book: The Squaw Valley Community of Writers on the Art of Fiction,* (Chronicle Books, 2007), 87.

Go Outside

are embedded in the natural world—whether it be the caves and wilderness of the early desert fathers and mothers or the fields and mountainsides of early monastic communities. There is something about being next to God's handiwork that enlivens the soul.

Tragically, our recent separation from nature prevents us from really feeling the increasing destruction and suffering that is occurring on the earth. Scientific observers tell us we are going through the greatest period of extinction ever experienced within the last 65 million years of this planet. We hear this, shake our heads, and then change the channel. As a friend who works for the Department of Fish and Game here in the state of Oregon recently said to me, "We think it's the environment that's in danger. The environment will eventually be fine. It might take a few million years, but it will recover. It's we humans who won't survive. Death of the environment is death to the earth's ability to sustain human life."

But again, all of this is abstract, futuristic, strange, and hard to comprehend. It's difficult to feel the suffering the earth is experiencing. It's difficult, for example, to feel or even care about the rapidly declining salmon population here in the Pacific Northwest when you haven't spent time wading in rivers or enjoyed potlucks abundant with fish from the fall salmon runs. When you don't know the smell, the sound, and the rhythms of a river, it simply becomes a political cause, an "issue" within "the environmental movement." Kids need to touch the real God within the real world, not only so they can bring their senses into prayer and be awakened not only to the wonder and mystery of God's creation, but also to the human ignorance and greed that is making God's world increasingly uninhabitable.

Youth ministers have always known the power of the outdoors to awaken the souls of young people. Teenagers need to be taken out from the carpeted, beige-colored, artificially lit, climate-controlled rooms of our churches. That's why youth ministry has traditionally relied upon backpacking trips, summer camps, recreational outings, beach bonfires, and snow excursions. Youth workers know, intuitively, that exposing kids to the natural world not only awakens the senses of young people, but also stirs and alerts the adolescent soul to the presence of God. The following exercises seek to deepen the way in which young people experience the created world—so every tree, mountain, lake, and river becomes not just a sign of God's presence but an occasion for prayer.

Prayer of the Senses

> Such love does the sky now pour, that whenever I
> stand in a field, I have to wring out the light when I
> get home.
> —ST. FRANCIS OF ASSISI

One way I like to introduce teenagers into a deeper experience of the natural world and God's presence within it is to invite them to pray through their senses. If we're sitting on a beach or hiking through a forest or cooling our feet in a stream or even simply lounging outside the church on a sunny day, I'll ask the young people to pay attention to what they see, hear, smell, and feel. If we're enfolded by nature, say on a mountain or in a forest, I'll ask them to sit somewhere alone and imagine that the smell of the trees, the sounds of the birds and creatures, and the feel of the wind are all God's seeking to love and be with them. If we're sitting outside the church and the sun is shining, I might have them lie back and imagine the warm sun is God's love seeking to know and heal them. I ask them to refrain from praying petitions, and simply notice the sun or wind or sound of the ocean as if it were God's love—and then see what happens. After 10 minutes or more I might invite them to pray to God whatever words come to them. Then we gather together and talk about the experience of seeking to be with God through the sights and sounds of nature.

This experience can also be powerful when visiting a place where a natural disaster has taken place or pollution is destroying the ecosystem. A friend of mine took his youth group to the coastline around New Orleans a few months after Hurricane Katrina had destroyed the city. Before they began a week of working to repair homes, he had his young people spread out across a beach littered with roof shingles, toys, drywall, broken furniture, clothing, and heaps of plastic bottles and garbage that had been washed out from the city and into the ocean. The kids sat and watched as the ocean waves carried Styrofoam, painted plywood, oil cans, and other objects from the destroyed homes and lives of New Orleans. Before sending them out, my friend asked the youth to pray with their eyes. To sit and just see and smell the results of the hurricane and then pray whatever words came to them.

Lectio Divina in Nature

In the same way that you might use a *lectio divina* approach to pray over the words of Scripture (see the exercise on *lectio divina* in chapter 8), you can invite teenagers to do *lectio* over the sights, sounds, and objects of nature. Here are the steps I follow when leading the *lectio divina* prayer in nature:

Preparation. Gather the youth together and explain the steps of the prayer. Talk about how Jesus spent much of his time outdoors and often found natural objects as signs and symbols of God's truth and presence. Explain that this prayer is a time of seeking to be with God through nature. Tell them how long the experience will last and give them some suggestions for handling distractions. Make sure you tell them the physical boundaries within which to explore their prayer (you don't want kids wandering too far) and tell them the sound or signal you'll use to call them back. Remind students to give their full attention to God in nature and try to refrain from interacting with others.

Opening. After answering any questions, lead the group in a simple opening prayer to dedicate the time to God. In prayer, thank God for the created world and ask God to open eyes, ears, hearts, and minds to God's truth and love. Then invite the youth to quietly notice their surroundings: You might say something like, "For a few moments just notice your surroundings, all that God has made—the meandering creek, the wind in the trees, the blue jays and their cries. What do you hear? What do you see? What do you feel in this place?" Pause for a few moments allowing students to enter into their surroundings.

Lectio. When the group seems ready, invite them to prayerfully walk and explore their surroundings. Tell them to pay attention to what draws their attention. I might say, "Notice what God is bringing to your attention. When something strikes you...a plant, a stone, a bird, whatever...allow yourself to stop, maybe even sit, and just be with whatever part of nature God is bringing to your attention. Don't force anything, just simply listen and look for a part of nature that seems to call for your attention."

Meditation. "What is God saying to you as you pray with this part of nature? Notice what thoughts, feelings, and images come to you as you pray with this part of nature. What is being offered?"

Prayer. "Express yourself in some way to God. Pray whatever feelings, desires, requests, or gratitudes have come to you in the prayer. Communicate your honest thoughts and feelings to Jesus or the Holy Spirit until there is nothing left to share."

Contemplation. "After a few minutes simply rest in God. Bask in whatever God has given you in this prayer. Allow yourself to rest in the midst of what God has created. Allow yourself to drop beneath all your thoughts and feelings and rest in the God who loves the whole world into being."

Testimony. I then walk around and gather the students back together. I invite them to share what took place in their prayer. Sometimes I'll give them time to journal before gathering them together. I try to give time so that as many students can share as possible.

Alone in the Wilderness

Henri Nouwen once wrote, "Solitude is the furnace of transformation."[17] It was outside, alone under the open sky of the desert, that Jesus first faced the temptations of the Accuser and affirmed God as the true Source of his identity. Throughout his ministry Jesus walked away from the needs and work of his ministry in order to spend time alone under the sun and moon, in prayer and reflection, centering himself in God's love.[18]

During retreats, weeklong camps, or mission trips, I sometimes send young people out along a lakeside, mountain, green field, or campground to spend an afternoon, a day, or even a whole night in prayer and reflection. Sometimes I send them with particular Bible passages to meditate on.[19] Often I encourage them to bring notebooks and pens so they can journal their prayers and thoughts to God. Before they go, I talk

---

[17] *The Way of the Heart: Desert Spirituality and Contemporary Ministry* (HarperCollins, 1991), 25.

[18] Here are just a few examples: Matthew 14:23; Mark 1:35; 6:31; Luke 5:16; 6:12; John 8:1; 10:40.

[19] I've found the following to be particularly fruitful: Psalms 8, 27, 139; Isaiah 6:1-9; 43:2-7; Matthew 6:5-8; Mark 6:30-44; 14:3-9; Luke 12:22-32; John 6:35-39; Romans 8:18-39; Ephesians 4:25-32.

about how Jesus would go out alone to pray—in the wilderness, in deserted places, in the mountains—to be renewed and connected to God's love. I then invite them to take walks, wade in the water (if we're near a lake, creek, or beach), nap in the grass, pray, read— while keeping a silent appreciation of God throughout all they do, as if Jesus were right next to them walking, praying, napping, and meditating on God's truth. When the time comes to a close, I bring them together and have them share about their experiences being outside in prayer and solitude.[20]

—◦◦◦—

If God is in all things, then it's possible to know and sense God every time we go out to pray in the world. Once when St. Francis was sitting in a forest speaking to an old squirrel about the sacraments, the squirrel got excited, ran into a hollow in his tree, and then returned holding some acorns, an owl feather, and a ribbon he had found. Francis smiled and said, "Yes, dear, you understand: Everything imparts God's grace."

[20] Two books that discuss solitude and prayer by Henri Nouwen that I've found helpful and given frequently to young people in my ministry: *Out of Solitude: Three Meditations on the Christian Life* (Ave Maria Press, 1974) and *The Way of the Heart: Desert Spirituality and Contemporary Ministry* (HarperCollins, 1991).

10 Rest

But he was in the stern, asleep on the cushion…
—MARK 4:38

Kids need sleep; kids don't get enough sleep. The result, according to neurologists, educators, and developmental psychologists, is that teenagers are tired and overstimulated and aren't getting the rest they need to develop healthy brains and bodies. Sleep deprivation results in weight gain, depression, diabetes, difficulties in school, even traffic accidents.[21]

One of my first discoveries in praying with teenagers is that young people fall asleep in prayer. (This shouldn't be surprising when, according to one study, more than half of

---

[21] "Sleep Deprivation May Be Undermining Teen Health," *Monitor on Psychology* volume 32, No. 9. October 2001. The article goes on to say, "Car accidents are the leading cause of death among adolescents, and safety experts believe drowsy driving is a major factor."

all students sleep seven hours or less, and almost one in five gets less than six hours of sleep a night.[22]) In reaction I tried to make sure any prayer exercises I used with students would keep them active and awake. But then I came across a little story of Abba Poeman, one of the ancient desert fathers from the fourth century. Abba Poeman was sitting in his room one day when a member of the community came to him and complained that many of the new members were falling asleep in chapel. Abba Poeman responded, "When I see a brother falling asleep, I move next to him, lay his head on my lap, and let him sleep."

After reading this story I began to wonder: *What if I designed retreats and exercises in which young people were encouraged to pray by sleeping?*

Holy Rest

One of the best ways we can help young people experience "holy leisure" is by giving kids time to sleep and nap. Most youth camps and retreats I attend are overscheduled. It's as if we really believe that idleness is the devil's playground. And yet how can young people absorb the teaching and presence of Jesus if they're constantly being hustled from one

[22] Study was done by Case Western Reserve University. "Homeroom Zombies," *Newsweek*, September 17, 2007, 64.

activity to another. Instead of creating a full schedule of events and presentations, try simplifying the
schedule. Give kids time to sleep in. Make time within Sunday school classes, camp outings, and youth
meetings for naps. Invite kids to see these times of
rest as prayer. Before kids go to bed at night, or before an afternoon nap, ask kids to dedicate the time
to God, to sense God in their breathing. Invite the
youth to sleep with the awareness that they are entering the peace and rest of God. Wake them with music
and talk with them. Ask them to reflect on their time
of prayerful sleep. See if they experience rest differently when they enter into it as a form of prayer.

—◦◦◦—

I explained this exercise at a national convention of
youth workers a year ago. After describing it, I invited the youth workers to take 30 minutes for "holy
napping." I passed out blankets and pillows while a
musician friend of mine played various lullaby-like
chants from the monastic community at Taizé. Thirty minutes later I woke the youth workers and asked
them to share their experiences. A young woman
from Zimbabwe spoke first. She told me she was very
angry when I first described the exercise. She had
flown thousands of miles to attend the convention.

Her congregation in Africa had spent thousands of dollars to send her to Los Angeles for the conference. When she heard me invite them to rest for 30 minutes as prayer, she said her face got "hot." She felt I was wasting her time and her church's money. But having nowhere else to go during that time, she begrudgingly accepted the invitation to rest and sleep.

When she awoke 30 minutes later, she noticed what she called "a strange peacefulness." She lay quiet for a few moments and then realized she was breathing "below the neck," for the first time in many months. At that moment she realized she was carrying lots of anger, stress, and tears that she'd been afraid to let herself feel. In Zimbabwe, she worked amid a community of young people who were HIV-positive. She said many of these youth were filled with fear, anger, and sadness. She described the young people she worked with as "lepers," ostracized from the community and sometimes separated from their own families. She spent much of her ministry organizing social and educational programs for these youth. But as she rested in God she realized that maybe what they needed most wasn't more Bible study, but instead a safe and welcoming place to sleep, relax, and feel God's peace within their ailing bodies.

What if kids came home from our camps and other youth ministry events rested? Young people always like to stay up late with friends, so what if you changed the schedule to allow the young people to sleep in? What if you blessed their sleeping in? What if you reminded them that the Scriptures are filled with people like Abraham, Jacob, Joseph, and Samuel who heard God in their sleep? What if you told them Jesus liked to sleep, that God commands us to get some rest, and that napping and sleeping are part of what it means to be a good Christian? What if you asked kids to pay attention to their dreams and listen for the ways in which God may be speaking to them?[23]

[23] Morton Kelsey, *Dreams: A Way to Listen to God*, (Paulist Press, 1978).

11 Imagine

I am about to do a new thing; now it springs forth,
do you not perceive it?
—ISAIAH 43:19

From Teresa of Avila, who was given an image of prayer as a castle with interior rooms, to the anonymous author of "Footprints" who wrote down a prayer experience in which she walked with Jesus on a sandy beach, Christians have long prayed with their imaginations. Julian of Norwich envisioned Jesus in his house throwing a feast for his friends, moving from person to person, "completely relaxed and courteous...radiating measureless love...that filled that place with joy and light." At six years old Catherine of Siena saw an image of God that made "the cheeks of the sun pale." It shouldn't be surprising that prayer engages the imagination, since most children are exposed to pictures and images that tell the story of Jesus long before they read the words of Jesus. Yet those of us raised in word-heavy, Protestant communions often have strong reservations about the use of images or imagination in prayer. Doesn't the Bible command us to refrain from creating images of God? Isn't the imagination susceptible to the devil?

Praying with our imagination isn't a form of idol-making. Nor is the imagination sinful or particularly susceptible to sin. Our imaginations are neutral. They can be used for good or for ill.[24] Imaginative prayer is the attempt to pray by using and interacting with images in the same way we commonly use words—as symbols of the God who lives beyond all forms of human depiction. Imaginative prayer is an experience of consecrating our God-given imaginative capacities in prayer. In imaginative prayer we invite God to use these creative capacities to help us develop a more intimate knowledge and loving attraction to the person of Jesus Christ.

We sometimes forget that, traditionally, Christians have most commonly known God through images. The Bible wasn't really widely read and available until

[24] The bombing of the World Trade Center, the cluster grenades used by U.S. soldiers in Iraq, and the gas ovens used in Nazi Germany all took imagination and creativity. And yet at the same time we see evidence of human imagination used in the service of God through the nonviolent tactics of the civil rights movement, the Truth and Reconciliation Commission in South Africa, and the hymns and music that give hope to people who are suffering. The real question is will human beings use their imaginations to destroy or to bless?

the advent of the printing press in the 16th century—and even then most people weren't educated enough to read it. Before the words of Scripture became accessible, most Christians contemplated the mysteries of faith as they found them portrayed in the frescoes, architecture, stained glass, statues, and woodcarvings placed in shrines and cathedrals. It was through these "bibles" that most people came to know Jesus long before they read the words and stories of Jesus in Scripture. Thus the common person's prayer was often rich with imagery and imagination.

Jesus also trust in the imaginations of people. His parables are invitations to listeners to imagine scenes and settings that communicate the truth and love of God. Each time Jesus tells a parable, he's saying, "Imagine a father had two sons..." or "Imagine a Samaritan saw a man hurt and bleeding in a ditch..." or "Imagine a man found a treasure in a field..." Jesus' parables inspire us to dream and picture and find ourselves within the stories and images that disclose the hidden reality of God.

As human beings, our first form of communication is through sight. We respond more to the facial expressions and gestures of a person than to the words that are being spoken. Imaginative prayer is powerful for adolescents because it invites them to respond emotionally as well as intellectually, and often cultivates an interior knowledge and affection for the person of Jesus Christ. When I introduce young people to imaginative prayer, a few students usually confess that they use imagination in prayer but have been unsure whether this is acceptable or normal.

I once did a research project on the use of active imagination in the prayer lives of teenagers. I led a number of youth groups in various forms of imaginative prayer and had the students journal their experiences. Here's the journal entry of one 15-year-old girl that expresses the kind of intimacy and transformation that can take place:

This was truly an amazing experience. I shut my eyes and focused on breathing as if God were being taken into me, filling me with light and peace and all pain was leaving. After a few moments I began to let go and relax. I listened to the Scripture passage. I walked with the disciples. When Jesus turned and asked them, "What are you looking for?" John 1:38 I answered, "Peace, love, courage, and to always believe." I kept asking.

I asked him to hold me, to drive all fear away, and imagined being held in his arms. He took me into the ocean, we soared above the earth, he told me I had courage and would move great mountains. I was free. Completely relaxed and felt magnificent—as if I were really being filled with his warmth and light. I didn't want to open my eyes, but when I did, I felt so much love, and peace. I felt speechless and so happy, my throat got choked up and my eyes stung as if I would cry…Thank you, Jesus.

Imaginative prayer can be assuring and comforting as well as convicting and reflective as seen in this journal entry from a 14-year-old girl:

I was going over the Scripture in my head, and a picture came to me. It was a picture of a wall, and Jesus was on the other side. I saw the other side. There was sunshine, green grass, and a rainbow. On my side there was a little grass by the wall but the rest was brown dirt. I began to sense that the Lord was trying to tell me…that there's a wall

that I have to overcome...Then a picture of my
sister came to mind. She's four years younger than
me. I have trouble keeping my temper when I'm
around her. I realized I need to really try.

Here are a few exercises I've used with teenagers in my ministries. Each of these exercises draws upon a student's imaginative capacity as a setting for prayer.[25]

Imaginative Contemplation

Following a debilitating war injury and a powerful experience of grace, Ignatius of Loyola heard a call from God to draw people into companionship with Jesus Christ and his mission of love. To do this, Ignatius began traveling throughout Spain teaching, preaching, and guiding those who were interested in various methods of prayer.[26] Over time Ignatius found that one of the most powerful methods for helping people receive and respond to Jesus was to imaginatively pray the Gospels. Ignatius discovered that when people were invited to prayerfully imagine a biblical story taking place, their response and connection to Jesus was more intimate, reflective, and transforming. Ignatius found that people were more easily drawn into contemplation of Jesus by gazing

[25] For other imaginative exercises with Scripture, see chapter 8.

[26] Ignatius would go on to found the Jesuit community and organize his method of Christian formation into a 30-day retreat referred to as the Spiritual Exercises of St. Ignatius of Loyola.

upon his actions in Scriptures than through other forms of prayer that relied solely on words, concepts, or petitions.

In my own study I've found Ignatian or imaginative contemplation to be particularly effective in helping young people come in contact and conformity with the person of Jesus Christ.[27] Here are the steps I follow when leading a group of young people in imaginative contemplation:

Preparation. After preparing the room for prayer I invite the young people to find places in the room where they feel they can pray comfortably. I then give a brief overview of the passage over which we will pray. For example, if our prayer were based on Luke 10:38-41, I might say something like: "The passage we'll be praying over takes place in a home. Jesus has been walking through towns, traveling and teaching, and then comes to a village where two sisters live. Their names are Mary and Martha. Martha invites Jesus to come to their home to rest and visit. Soon after Jesus enters the home, Martha begins to work and prepare drinks and food; meanwhile her sister Mary goes over, sits at Jesus' feet, and listens intently to what he's saying. Martha interrupts and says to Jesus, 'Lord, don't you care that my sister is leaving all the work for me? Tell her to help me out.'

---

[27] Drive to Berkeley, California, and look up my thesis at the Graduate Theological Union library in which I documented the experiences of 100 teenagers with Ignatian contemplation. It's titled "Ignatian Contemplation and the Process of Adolescent Spiritual Formation." Then have a cup of coffee around the corner at Brewed Awakening.

Jesus turns to Martha and basically says, 'Martha, Martha, you are worried and distracted by many things. Mary's made the better choice.'

Instruction. I then explain how the prayer will proceed. I say something like, "In a moment I'm going to help us quiet ourselves for prayer, and then I'm going to read this Bible passage. As I read it I want you to imagine yourself watching the story. I want you to allow yourself to see the sisters, hear them talking, smell the food cooking, and watch Jesus respond to them. You may find, as you imagine the story, that you become one of the sisters or that you're one of the disciples sitting in the back of the room or maybe that you're just yourself working in the kitchen with Martha. As I read the story and in the silence that follows, let your imagination go where it will. Don't try to force anything, just allow the images and story to unfold. During this part of the prayer, things might happen that aren't in the story. You and Jesus might come into the kitchen and start making food. You and Martha might get angry and stomp out of the house and then sit under a tree talking. Just be open to what happens and don't try to force it or control it. We're offering this time to God, we're offering our imaginations to God; let's see what the Holy Spirit has to teach us." I then tell them how long the silence will last and let them know I'll call them together to share their experiences at the close of the prayer.

Center. I invite the young people to sit for a moment and let the tensions and activity of the day fall off them as if they were removing a heavy jacket. I then remind them that God is not only with us, but also within us. I invite them to spend a few moments of silence reflecting on the mysterious truth that God's life-giving presence is in their bodies, in their minds, and in their hearts.

Desire. After a few minutes of quiet, I invite the young people to offer themselves—their bodies, their minds, their thoughts and desires to Jesus or to God. I ask them to dedicate this time to God. I might say something like, "What is one deep longing that you want to bring to Jesus at this time? Keep this desire close to you as we enter into prayer."

Read. I then begin reading the passage. I read it slowly, pausing from time to time so there's room for the prayer of the young people to develop. At times I give prompts or questions to help the students engage their senses within the prayer. For example if I'm reading the story of Jesus' visit to Mary and Martha's home, I might begin by reading Luke 10:38, "Now as they went on their way, he entered a certain village, where a woman named Martha welcomed him into her home," and then pause and ask, "What do you notice as Jesus enters the village with his friends? What does the village feel and smell like?" Pause. "What do you hear, what do you see as Martha comes to Jesus and welcomes him into her home? Take a few moments to follow Jesus into the home of Martha and Mary. Notice what it feels like to be in this home." After pausing, I read the next verse followed by a few more prompts and silences to allow their prayer to move and breathe.

Silence. After reading the entire passage, I allow five to 10 minutes of silence depending on the setting and the group.

Gratitude. At the end of the time of silence, I invite the young people to offer thanks to God for whatever has occurred in the prayer and then to gently bring their attention back to the room.

Testimony. I often like to pass out pencils and paper and allow the kids to spend a few minutes journaling over the prayer. Then I gather the group together and ask them to share their experiences. Some youth will have profound experiences. Some might feel like they really encountered Jesus. Other students will stare blankly and, when asked, will tell you they didn't feel or see a thing. Others will tell you they fell asleep. Again, it's important to let these kids know that everyone has times when they just can't pray; or it may be that this form of prayer just isn't right for them right now. I tell kids that when they're in a prayer exercise that seems flat or empty, they can simply say to God, "God, I want to be with you" and let that be enough. I remind them that the desire to be with God and to seek God is more pleasing to God than any prayer method.

We can create many different settings in which young people can interact with Jesus: In the temple of Jerusalem when Jesus is 12 years old and has just escaped his parents; as he sits in Mary and Martha's house preparing to eat a meal; while he prays by himself on a mountain after feeding the five thousand; while sitting in a boat after calming a storm; while he sits among children holding and blessing them; while he hangs on a cross; bleeding and dying; or his resurrection appearance to the disciples on the Sea of Tiberias, where he sits on the beach grilling fish and bread. It's important to give cues and prompts to help the young people see and feel the setting. Sometimes, as in the example above, it's important to have particular questions or a focus when asking them to engage Jesus. Sometimes you can take these questions directly from Jesus: "Who do you say that I am?" or "What do you want me to do for you?" or "Why did you doubt?" In all these various settings we can encourage young people to respond to Jesus with their words and emotions.

Praying Our Lives

Some forms of imaginative prayer are autobiographical, inviting us to use the episodes and experiences of our lives as the source of prayer. You'll find the words and process I use for three possible examples of this kind of prayer described below. After preparing a room for prayer, invite youth to imaginatively pray over one of the following:

Experiencing Love[28]

You might lead this prayer by saying something like, "Ask God to remind you of a time when you felt deeply loved. Maybe it was a time as a child or a time as recent as today. Some moment when you felt deeply loved and appreciated. What was taking place? How was this love shown to you? Were there words, gestures, or an act of some sort? How did you feel? Remember as much of the scene as you can. For the next few moments try to remember and savor the feeling of this experience of being loved." (Pause one to three minutes.)

"Now, while you are remembering this time, turn and ask God, 'How were you present in this experience?' For the next few moments seek to find

[28] This prayer is a modified version of an exercise in Anthony de Mello's *Sadhana: A Way to God* (Image, 1984), 72.

the presence of God in this scene. In what way was God present?" (Allow five minutes of silence.)

"Now take a moment to thank God for whatever you've noticed in your prayer. Then when you're ready, turn your attention back to the room."

Seeing Our Gifts[29]

To lead a prayer experience focused on realizing one's gifts, I might say something like, "Imagine that Jesus wakes you late one night and invites you to watch your own life. You watch yourself wake up, get dressed, and go to school. You observe yourself in your classroom and with your friends. What is it like to watch yourself go through a normal day? What do you notice about yourself? What do you like about yourself?" (Pause one minute.)

"After watching your daily life, Jesus invites you to see yourself through the eyes of others. First, Jesus allows you to step inside the body of a good friend. Take a moment to see yourself through that person's eyes. What's one thing he or she seems to like about you?" (Pause one minute.)

"Now imagine that Jesus invites you to look through the eyes of a close family member with whom you get along well. Take a moment to see

[29] Modified from a prayer titled "Good Things" by Mark Link in *Prayer Paths: Search for Serenity and God in an Age of Stress* (Tabor, 1990), 82-83.

yourself through that person's eyes. What's one thing your friend values in you?" (Pause one minute.)

"Now imagine that Jesus invites you to see yourself through his eyes. Take a moment to see yourself through the eyes of Jesus. What does God value in you? What does Jesus like about you?" (Pause one minute.)

"Finally, Jesus takes you back to your home. What is it you want to say to him as he brings you back from this experience? Talk to Jesus as a friend about what you've seen in this experience. What does it mean for your life?"

Healing a Hurt

A third exercise in praying our lives invites students to open the painful moments in their lives to God's healing. This particular exercise can draw up lots of hurt and pain within young people. Be prepared to have plenty of time to debrief the exercise and respond to kids who have new insights into past wounds. Here are the words I often use in leading this experience:

"Imagine you are in a sacred room within your own heart. The room is like a chapel lit with candles. In this room are images and objects that represent the deepest moments of your life. Some objects come from your childhood—pictures of loved ones, gifts given to you, things from nature that you played with as a child. You walk around the room noticing all the different symbols and objects that have shaped and formed your heart." (Pause for two minutes.)

"After exploring the different objects in the room you notice that Jesus is standing next to you. He takes your hand and leads you to a wooden box. He opens the box and inside are symbols and objects of past hurts and pain. He invites you to take one of these objects out. You're reluctant at first, but eventually you reach in and take out an image or object that represents a past injury. Jesus asks you to tell him how this hurt. For the next few moments tell Jesus all you know about it." (Pause for three minutes.)

"As you look up at Jesus, you see he is listening to you with care and compassion. Jesus then asks if he can hold this suffering for you. You reach out your hand and give it to him to hold. For the next few moments you notice what it's like to let Jesus hold this suffering for you." (Pause for three minutes.)

"After holding this wound, Jesus walks you to a small altar, in the center of your heart. On that altar is a cross. Jesus lays your suffering on the altar then takes your hand and walks you out from the center of your heart, out into a green grassy field and bright sunshine. You lie back on the grass and stare up at the blue sky. You feel the warmth of the sun on your face. And suddenly you feel light as air. For the next few moments, communicate to God the prayers of your heart. Then, when you're ready, bring your attention back to the room."

There are many other exercises you can undertake with youth that invite them to review their lives with God. It can be very powerful for young people to engage in a prayer exercise in which they imagine their own funerals and the words of regret and blessing people might express about their lives. Other prayers might invite them to go into the future and see God's hopes for them. Young people often find prayers that invite them to draw on their own experiences to be more accessible than other forms of imaginative prayer.

Images of Blessing

In the nightly prayers of Teresa of Avila, she made a habit of remembering everyone she had seen that day. Sometimes when we are praying for someone, we picture that person in our prayer. We gaze upon that individual, sensing his or her pain with love and empathy. To visualize a person enfolded in God's love is another way of practicing intercession. I particularly like to use this prayer when youth are gathered to pray for someone who is hurting or in need.

After helping the youth settle themselves for prayer, invite them to picture someone who needs their prayers. Maybe it is a friend or someone who is sick or hurting. Maybe it is a series of people, such as Iraqi civilians suffering in the war or children who are forced to work in sweatshops making tennis shoes. You might invite students to picture an enemy or someone with whom they're angry. After a few moments of silence, invite the young people to picture this person surrounded by God's light. Without using words, simply see this person being healed and blessed by God's light and love. After a few moments of quiet, invite the youth to speak to God whatever words or petitions might come to them.

On service trips it's great to gather the youth at the end of the day and have them, like Teresa of Avila, go through their day and picture, unhurriedly, everyone they've encountered. Invite the youth to bless these people in their praying imagination by touching each of them—maybe with a hug, a touch of hands, or by placing a hand on their heads. Encourage the youth to see themselves touching and blessing everyone they've encountered. Then close by gathering the group together and having them speak aloud whatever names or petitions come to them.

———❧———

God seeks to live in all aspects of our being—in our thoughts, our hopes, our hurts, our desires and dreams. When we invite young people to open their imaginations to God, they can find a new source of comfort and inspiration. Human imagination is a powerful faculty—it can stir us to feel empathy, drive us to act, inspire us to engage in creative acts of love, and comfort us so we can bear the suffering of this life.

In his book *The Spiritual Life of Children*, psychologist Robert Coles documented the prayers and spiritual life of a 12-year-old named Leola. Leola had become a paraplegic in a car accident that took the life of her father. Coles first encountered Leola in the 1960s when she lived with her mother in a black working-class neighborhood. According to Coles, Leola was not a "bright child"—her test scores were below average. She loved to spend time with children and babies, crawling on the floor alongside them. However her spiritual life was particularly inspiring. Leola, according to Coles, loved to pray. "I pray sitting [in the chair], and I pray lying [on the bed], but most of all, I pray on the floor, holding on to the bed, my poor knees doing the best they can to bend."

Kneeling was difficult for Leola; she had to use her powerful torso and arms to get down from a chair, move across the floor, pull herself up alongside the bed, and hold herself upright in a kneeling position. Coles felt it was only her passion and her "mind's eager yearning" that gave Leola the patience and persistence it took to arrange herself on her unfeeling knees for prayer. Once she got her body arranged she would hum, tell God her "down-and-out-blues," ask for forgiveness, and offer thanks for her life. Sometimes, however, there was another experience. Leola explained, "The praying goes to my head, and I gets lost, I think—it's like, well, He comes and takes me, and I'm no longer thinking and talking, I'm just someplace else, I don't know where. I can even look down from there, and I see poor little me, Leola and her bed, and the chair is there, too..." In these brief moments of sensing Jesus near, these prayerful moments when she was watching and seeing her room and her broken body, she would sometimes feel whole again and see herself "walking like I used to walk—walking," as she told Dr. Coles, "to meet Jesus."[30]

[30] Houghton Mifflin, 1990, 200-201.

12 Eat

> Listen! I am standing at the door, knocking; if you hear my voice and open the door, I will come in to you and eat with you, and you with me.
>
> —REVELATION 3:20

In the fellowship hall of Lake Chelan Lutheran Church in Washington, 20 students and five adults sit hungrily along the outer edge of a hexagon of tables. It's dinnertime, and the air is rich with the smell of a good meal. Pastor Paul Palumbo steps out from the kitchen, drying his hands on a dish towel, and says, "Welcome, everyone. You guys are in for a real treat. Martha Linton is a longtime church member and great cook, and she's made dinner for all of us tonight." He turns back toward the kitchen and calls, "Martha, will you tell everyone what you've prepared?"

A slightly stooping, grandmotherly figure in a red apron comes out from behind the counter and smiles at the group, "Well, let's see. I wasn't sure what you all would eat, so I asked my husband, George. He told me to make Swedish meatballs. I think he said that because it's his favorite, and he figured there'd be leftovers. I've made some rice and a salad and some extra gravy. I also threw together some blackberry pies for dessert. I hope you like it."

Paul takes Martha's hand and invites us all to stand in a circle and hold hands. We shift and shuffle until we're all linked and looking at one another. Paul takes his time, waiting for conversations to quiet. "Let's give thanks," Paul calls us to prayer while closing his eyes and bowing his head. Fifty eyes close and 25 heads bow in response. In a steady cant, Paul thanks God for Martha and her work preparing the meal. He thanks God for the earth and the food it yields. He thanks God for the young people and adults who have gathered. He then asks that all of us might be aware of Jesus' presence around the table.

Slowed by grace, we quietly pick up plates and line up to receive George's favorite meal. After we sit, I notice the kids approaching their food cautiously. No one is familiar with Swedish meatballs.

The boy next to me takes his fork, cuts the meatball open, and peers inside.

He scrunches his nose in uncertainty and asks, "Do you know what's in this?" I shrug my shoulders. The boy raises his fork toward his mouth, gives it the sniff test, and then places the food inside. He glances upward, focusing his concentration on the sensations in his mouth. A smile of relief spreads across his face. He turns to me and says with delight, "It's good!"

The students and volunteers in Lake Chelan's youth ministry return to the counter for seconds, and then thirds, until Martha says laughingly, "It looks like poor George isn't going to get any leftovers!" After the main meal comes the blackberry pies, made from berries Martha handpicked from her own yard. One boy tells Martha it's the first time he's ever had homemade pie. Another pipes up that he's had pie lots of time, "But this is the best." Determined to trump this claim, a senior girl cries out, "This isn't just the best pie; this is the best *dessert* I've ever had." Martha beams from the kitchen doorway and tells the young lady she'll teach her how to make it some time.

The scene could not have been more different two weeks later, when I was a visiting speaker for a youth group outside Los Angeles. I arrived early and received a tour of the church's youth ministry facilities. After seeing the gym, the classrooms, the recreation room, and the youth ministry offices, the youth director proudly points to what he calls, "The best thing in our youth facility." There, in the back of the youth room is a soda dispenser. The same kind of dispenser you'd find at most fast-food restaurants. "We've got a guy in our church who works as a soda distributor. He got us an amazing discount. It's been the greatest evangelism tool we've ever had. Kids tell their friends, "Come to youth group, you get all the pop you want free!"

Thirty minutes later the kids arrive and immediately crowd around the dispenser. A group of guys are so enthusiastic about the free soda that they chug their first cup in seconds, then quickly push their way back in for a refill. When the youth director finally invites me to speak, I go to the front of the room and look out at the 50 kids and adults, each sipping from a red Coca-Cola cup.

If there is one health hazard in youth ministry, it's the food. Pizza, cookies, soda, and fast-food hamburgers are mainstays among most of the kids we work with. Youth (and children) in North America are trained to eat high-sodium, sugary, highly processed, fatty, convenience foods. The result is that American youth are becoming increasingly unhealthy, with growing numbers suffering from diabetes and other nutrition-related illnesses.[31] In youth ministry we seek to live among young people. The unfortunate result, as Tony Jones comments in *Soul Shaper*, is that "a lot of youth workers are overweight."

In the Christian faith, eating is a sacred practice. God gave manna to the wandering tribe of Israel. Jesus ate with sinners and tax collectors as a sign of God's grace and friendship. He prepared food for his friends on the last night of his life and broke bread with many of his followers after he rose from the dead. To this day we talk of Jesus as the bread of life. It is through gathering around a table and sharing bread and wine together that Christians seek to embody the Spirit and life of Jesus.

Food is a sacred gift from God, a sign of God's care and love for human beings. As the psalmist writes, "You cause the grass to grow for the cattle, and plants for people to use, to bring forth food from the earth, and wine to gladden the human heart, oil to make the face shine, and bread to strengthen the human heart" (Psalm 104:14-15). God gives us food to "gladden the human heart." As followers of a savior who turned

---

[31] There are many articles on this subject. For a nice summary on the use of soft drinks by teens and its effect on teen health see "Nutritionists: Soda Making Americans Drink Themselves Fat" by Caleb Hellerman, www.cnn.com, September 18, 2007.

water into wine and compared the kingdom of God to a feast, Christians should be the one religion that knows how to party.

So what does it mean when the eating practices within our ministries mimic the culture to such a degree that we're actually contributing to the physical sickness of the youth we serve? What does it mean when we continually feed kids food that "clogs" rather than "gladdens" the hearts of youth? Youth ministry not only needs to teach the theology and beliefs of Christianity, it needs to help young people practice a different way of living, a rhythm of life that mirrors the health and richness that God yearns for us to experience. One way we help young people break free of a death-dealing culture of consumption is by helping them recover the sacred and pleasurable act of eating good food.

Grace

Gathering kids together to say a blessing over a meal is a simple yet beautiful way to communicate the gratitude and awareness Christians seek to embody. "If the only prayer you knew was, 'Thank you,' it would be enough," Meister Eckhart once said. As we invite young people to pause and give thanks before eating, we help communicate to young people an awareness of God in the most basic and intimate of human activities. How might you begin to see "saying grace" each time you ate together—whether before snacks, on a picnic, or over breakfast on a mission trip—as a way of slowing kids down, giving them a sense of God's rest and peace? How could the few minutes of blessing the food be a time of modeling and teaching prayer?

In one youth group I directed, we began every youth meeting with a 30-minute meal. We'd set the table and eat family style with a salad, a main course, and dessert. Each of these dinners began with the whole group standing, holding hands, and saying grace. In these opening blessings we took time to give thanks for the food, the people who prepared it, and the people who were about to receive it. And like my friend Paul Palumbo, we'd ask the Holy Spirit to keep each of us mindful of Christ's presence during our conversation.

Kids rarely eat home-cooked meals around a table anymore. Instead of buying packaged and processed food, why not invite members of your congregation to fix meals for the young people of your church? I've found that sitting around a table, eating a meal family style, not only communicates the kind of care and community the Christian faith seeks to embody, it also becomes a setting for good conversation. When the table is set with care, the prayer and blessing over that table carries on into the meal.

After the food is prepared gather students together to pray. There are many ways to do this. One of my favorite ways is to have them all stand and hold hands or sit around a table. Ask the youth to remain in silence, and simply make eye contact with each person, just seeing and acknowledging each person around the circle. Don't make this too precious. The silence and eye contact may feel awkward for some kids, and they will be tempted to smile or laugh. If they do, just smile back and continue to make eye contact with the other members of the group. This silence and seeing can be a powerful experience of slowing down, being present, and noticing the other people in the group.

When it feels like everyone has had a chance to look and see one another, ask the group to bow their heads for prayer. Then say a simple prayer, giving appropriate thanks for the kids, the group, the workers who prepared the food, etc. Leave some silences, some space between words to help everyone slow down. Then ask God to help the group notice God's presence in the food and conversation around the table.

If you eat together regularly, from time to time, you might close the mealtime by asking the kids, "So, did anyone notice how God was with us during our meal?"

Taste and See

"O taste and see that the Lord is good," says Psalm 34:8. This exercise invites youth to do that literally—focusing on the sense of taste as a way of widening their awareness and gaining a sense of prayer and God's presence in the food they eat. You can engage young people in this form of prayer as part of a meal or snack time with delicious, wholesome food.

Begin by setting out a table of delicious-looking food. Grapes, melon, apples, berries, home-baked bread or pastries, fresh juices. Avoid packaged or processed food. You may want to place all these foods on a table in advance, but leave them covered with a white tablecloth while you explain the exercise.

Discuss with the youth the fact that God wants us to eat and be fed. God provides us with food that not only satisfies but delights. God provided manna to the people of Israel; Jesus often used the image of a feast to communicate the kingdom of God. Christians share bread and wine at Communion as a way to remember and embody Jesus and his mission of love. Food is a gift and a sign of God's love. You might have young people share an experience of a special meal. Who was there? What took place? How was food important to this occasion?

Begin the exercise with a time of silence, in which you invite the young people to pray within themselves, offering this time to God. Then uncover the feast table, and explain that each student is to approach the table in silence and choose something to eat. Have them go someplace around the room or outside to eat. As they eat, invite them to receive this food as a gift from God to them. Ask them to imagine that God has prepared this food especially for them. Invite them to notice the texture, the smell, and the feel of this food in their mouths. For a few moments invite them to just eat the food with a sense of God's delight and pleasure—no words are necessary. Let the pleasure of eating be their prayer.

After they've finished eating, ask them to pray to God whatever thoughts, feelings, or images come to them. It may be a prayer of thanks for the food, a petition for those who are hungry, or a deep sense of gratitude for the workers who harvested or prepared the food.

Gather the group together and invite them to share their experiences. What did they notice in the prayer? What was it like to pray by eating? What was God like in the prayer? How might this prayer expand into their daily life?

Sometime after you've done this exercise, have the youth gather for Communion. This could take place at a regular Sunday morning service or you might prepare a special Eucharist service with the youth. Have the youth pray and seek "communion" with God while they taste the bread and juice.

Healthy Fasting

Throughout Christian history, countless people of faith have engaged in the traditional spiritual practice of fasting. Many praying Christians have found that fasting focuses the mind and opens the heart, helping the pray-er to recognize his or her own fragility and dependence on God. In my own experience, I've found that fasting helps me slow down and draw my attention to matters of the Spirit; the hunger I feel in my body while fasting begins to merge with my own hunger for God.

Over the years I've led many fasting experiences with adults and youth: Youth group fasts such as the "24-Hour Famine" to raise awareness and money for the hungry; daylong fasts to help young people focus their prayers and awareness of God; an intensive three-day fast in the wilderness to help youth through a rite of passage into adulthood. I've found these fasts to be fruitful for the adults and youth who participated. However, at the same time, I've had concerns that fasting can reinforce and give spiritual approval to many of the eating disorders afflicting so many young people. In much of North America, kids are tormented by images and messages that encourage overeating while simultaneously glorifying celebrities and models whose bodies are incredibly thin and sometimes even emaciated. The result is an epidemic of eating disorders. My suspicions about how fasting can play a role in this destructive cycle were confirmed when I asked a group of young people to write down their motivations for participating in an event in which the group would be invited to fast. Many of the young women wrote "to lose weight." At that point I realized I could no longer promote fasting as a spiritual practice to use with teens. In spite of precautions and great care, there is too great a risk that young people might get the message that purging, undereating, overexercising, and other forms of "beauty-ascetics" are the way to gain the love and approval of God and others.

Perhaps instead of fasting from food, you might encourage kids to fast from unhealthy foods—potato chips, fast food, and soda. You could encourage your young people to eat good and simple foods for a month, a week, or even just a day, and to spend meal times as prayer, seeking to receive God's love and life through eating healthy meals.

Prayerful Feasting

My wife started a "Slow Food" group when we lived in California.[32] Slow Food groups all over the world gather regularly to eat local, seasonal, organic, home-cooked meals. The emphasis is on enjoying good food, raising awareness of local farmers and food producers, and spending unhurried time in conversation around a table. On one Slow Food excursion, our group went out to a local strawberry farm, talked to the growers, and picked baskets of berries. Then we spent the whole afternoon picnicking amid a grove of redwoods.

What if you took your students out to a local farm and picked food together? Once you get out to the fields, you could read Psalm 104, which reminds us that it is God who brings "forth food from the earth." Have the kids pick food in silence, seeking to pray and attend to God's Spirit among fruit trees and vegetable plants. Then bring everyone back to the church to prepare a meal together. Bless it and eat it

---

[32] Slow Food is a nonprofit, "eco-gastronomic" organization founded in 1989 to counteract fast food and fast life, the disappearance of local food traditions, and people's dwindling interest in the food they eat, where it comes from, how it tastes, and how our food choices affect the rest of our world. For more information see www.slowfood.com.

unhurriedly, enjoying the pleasure of one another's company over a good meal.

In the unique faith community of Holden Village in north central Washington state, community members eat a simple meal (e.g., rice and beans) once a week as someone reads aloud the situation of hungry and hurting people from different parts of the world while the others remain in silence. Following the meal, community members gather at tables to write letters, petitioning organizations or elected officials to respond to the needs of hungry people. I've visited Holden Village several times with high school youth groups and found this simple, sacred meal to be particularly meaningful. This practice can also be adapted for use with your own group.

I must confess that, as a youth minister and parent, I've taken kids to fast-food outlets many times, served packaged cookies at countless youth meetings, and had hundreds of interactions with kids while drinking soda pop. Sometimes these "convenience foods" just make sense. I don't follow a strict diet, and I do indulge in high-fat foods from time to time (I'm Italian, after all, and make a mean Bolognese sauce).

However, over the past 12 years, I've struggled to create ministries (and a family life) that reflect the health and richness of life God seeks to offer us. If Jesus offers us life in abundance, shouldn't the eating and drinking practices of our youth groups also be filled with care and life? My prayer is that the people who come into our churches and ministries will sense that the Christian faith is different from the fast-food culture that surrounds it—that there is care, gratitude, and health, not only in what we believe, but also in how we live.

13 Befriend

Do not neglect to show hospitality to strangers, for
by doing that some have entertained angels without
knowing it.

—HEBREWS 13:2

Six months ago I was invited to travel to Guatemala to lead
a retreat for artists and staff who partner with Compassion
International, a Christian organization that provides food,
clothing, health care, and schooling to children suffering
from poverty.[33] On the last night of our retreat, we were introduced to a 22-year-old Maya woman named Auri, who
told us her story. Auri spent the early years of her childhood
in desperate poverty. Abandoned by her father, she and her
mother lived on the edge of the main garbage dump of Gua-

[33] Find out more about Compassion International and how you or your youth group can sponsor a child at
www.compassion.com.

temala City. Every morning she and her mother, along with hundreds of other people, would sort through the city refuse, collecting food, clothing, and any objects they could repair, refurbish, or sell. It was a dangerous life—Auri and her mother were often injured by broken glass and shards of metal, or infected by various toxins and bacteria found within the mounds of waste.

When Auri was 10 years old, her mother enrolled her in public school, seeking to give her a better life. Auri was required to bring her own writing utensils and paper, so her resourceful mother repaired a discarded school backpack, then filled it with recycled pencils, pens, and notebooks she had collected. Auri was nervous but excited to leave the garbage fields and join other children in school.

On the first day of class the teacher asked the students to introduce themselves. After Auri stood and gave her name, another student informed the class that Auri lived at the dump, and then called her a name that meant "trash." For the rest of the day the kids in the class taunted her, calling her "trash." That night Auri cried to her mother and told her she no longer wanted to attend school. But her mother was determined. So Auri went the next day and again experienced the name-calling and taunts of her classmates. After a month of tears, her mother finally relented and allowed Auri to withdraw from school. For the next three years she remained isolated in the dump, working beside her mother, trying to ward off hunger.

One day while she was scavenging the trash piles, a group of teenagers came to Auri and introduced themselves. They told her they were part of a new Christian school that was being formed near the dump. They invited Auri to come to a youth gathering that night. Auri refused the invitation, fearing it would be a repeat experience of the shaming and rejection she experienced in her previous attempt at schooling. Despite her refusal, the teenagers returned the following week. They spent an afternoon talking and helping her sort garbage. At the end of the afternoon they again invited her to attend the new Christian school. Although she found the students friendly, Auri refused to risk entering a situation in which she might suffer further humiliation. For the next six months these students found Auri, talked with her, helped her in her work, and invited her to attend the school. Each time she refused. Then one of the students told her there would be food at the meeting. She and her mother were having a very hard time. Neither of them had eaten in three days and were suffering terribly from hunger. Auri agreed to attend the meeting that night, not because she was interested in school, but because she felt she wouldn't survive another day without something to eat. That night Auri walked into town feeling certain she would be recognized at this new school as one of the "garbage people" and again would face ridicule and rejection. But she was so hungry she could no longer protect her pride.

Auri arrived at the gathering of teenagers at the new school. She quickly made her way to a table of pastries, fruit, and sandwiches. Trying not to reveal her hunger, she ate discreetly, carefully hiding extra sandwiches and fruit under her clothes to take to her mother. Her hunger satiated, Auri visited with the other students. She toured the new school facility, listened to music, and participated in a variety of social games. When the evening ended, she realized her face felt strange. She'd been smiling, something she rarely did in her daily life.

At the end of the evening, the students who had befriended Auri encouraged her to sign up for classes at the school. They assured her there would be no financial expense. Auri appreciated the invitation, but refused. Her impression of school as a place of humiliation was far too deep. She thanked her hosts and then turned to start home, her mind replaying all the pleasures of the evening—the friends, the food, the music, the laughter. As she was walking home savoring the evening, she had an epiphany. "It came to me so strongly that I had to stop and sit down right in the middle of the road," she told us. "I suddenly realized that the whole time I was at the school everyone called me by my name. My mind was filled with the faces of all of these people, many of them close to my own age. No one called me 'garbage girl'; no one called me 'trash.' Everyone called me by name." She looked at us intently, "Every one of them called me Auri."

Auri poured tears after she spoke these last lines—Auri, who now lives in an apartment in Guatemala City; Auri, who has held a job as a court stenographer and is now on her way to finishing her college degree; Auri, who now returns to the trash heaps of Guatemala City on weekends, befriending the children and young people who still live there, inviting them to attend the same Christian school that had saved her life. Auri gathered herself together and looked at us, her eyes still full of pain and gratitude and said, "Do you how beautiful it is to have people look at you and call you by your name?"

Something is missing when young people learn prayer as a private activity that exists only between an individual and God. To enter the life of prayer is to seek to have our eyes and ears touched by Jesus so we can see the presence of God in the person standing across the room, the stranger on the sidewalk, or the homeless girl in the garbage dump. Much of my time in youth ministry has been spent helping teenagers build community and practice hospitality to others (within the ministry as well as within the larger community).[34] One way we help our students open their hearts to others is by helping kids hold one another in prayer.

It is through prayer that Christian care and community move from mental concepts to realities of the heart. Prayer makes us vulnerable to others. It's difficult to cling to our defenses, our prejudices, and even our anger at another person when we're praying for them. The more we pray for someone, even an enemy, the more God softens the heart toward that person—the more that person changes from enemy to friend. Prayer makes it more likely that we can move from seeing someone as "garbage" to actually seeing the person as a child of God.

How do we help young people pray in a way that creates hospitality within them? How do we invite young people to see prayer as a practice that seeks to be mindful of the lives and suffering of others? Here

---

[34] Check Wayne Rice's *Up Close and Personal: How To Build Community in Your Youth Group* (Youth Specialties, 1989) for exercises in creating friendship and community within a ministry.

are three practices I use with youth for developing the awareness of others in the midst of prayer.

Practicing the Presence of Others

My friend "Fitz" works at St. Anthony's dining hall in the Tenderloin district of San Francisco. He's in charge of handling arrangements for various groups, mostly church and youth groups, who seek to volunteer at St. Anthony's kitchen and homeless shelter.[35] St. Anthony's serves more than 2,500 meals a day and provides counseling, shelter, health care, and employment services to thousands of people who suffer from addiction, poverty, and physical or mental disabilities. I remember the first time I met Fitz. I wanted to provide a day of real Christian service for a group of 100 teenagers. We were going to spend a day talking about Christ's call to serve the poor, and I thought it would be fitting to then have the students work in a kitchen preparing food, cleaning dishes, wiping tables, and handing out meals to those in need. St. Anthony's seemed like the perfect place to make this happen.

I drove into San Francisco and spent an afternoon touring the facilities; then I told Fitz my grand plan for teaching kids about serving the poor. Fitz, a Franciscan who had spent much of his life serving

[35] www.stanthonysf.org

the poor, looked at me kindly and then offered, "It might be more transforming to have your students befriend the poor rather than simply serve them anonymously." I knew instantly that Fitz was right. I had already participated in many service projects with youth in which it seemed in some ways that the people we were serving were actually being exploited—used as props to make the church, the young people, and the ministry leaders feel good about themselves. To befriend the poor was much more radical, would make us much more vulnerable. I asked Fitz how he proposed we do this. "The same way Jesus befriended people—you eat with them."

Later that summer I helped drive 100 teenagers into the heart of San Francisco. We parked behind St. Anthony's, gathered in a circle, and prayed that God would open our eyes so we might look at the people around us as if we were looking upon the face of Jesus.[36] I had the students pair up, gave them marking pens, and asked each of them to draw a simple cross on the back of one hand. I suggested they say a little prayer within themselves each time they noticed that cross: "God, help me see your face in the face of the person next to me." We then walked out in front of the dining hall.

[36] See Matthew 25:31-46.

It was lunchtime, and people from all over the neighborhood were lining up. I had the students stagger themselves throughout the serpentine line. The students talked in line with the other people who were waiting. Finally they were served lunch by St. Anthony's staff, and spent an hour sitting and dining with people, most of whom lived on the streets. When the meal ended, we gathered in a nearby chapel to share stories about the people we'd met. We talked about what it was like to hold these people in prayer as we were visiting with them. Many of us, including me, felt surprised at how similar we were to the people we'd met.

We help young people become blessed by those they serve by encountering the needy with prayerful hearts. What might it mean to have your students practice the presence of God among those who are in need? As Jean Vanier once wrote, "The promise of Jesus is to help us discover that the poor are a source of life and not just objects of our charity."[37]

We can help young people become sources of life not only by practicing prayer, but also by engaging others with prayerful hearts. It's what Brother Lawrence liked to call "practicing the presence of God." We can ask our young people to try to interact with others (on work trips, in youth group, in their

[37] *Community and Growth* (Paulist Press, 1989), 142.

schools and homes) with a sense that each person is created in the image of God. Gather students before school and have them draw crosses on the backs of their hands. Then ask them to go through their day seeking to be mindful of the presence of God within each person they meet. Let the crosses on their hands be reminders that Jesus seeks to be present within each person. Talk with them at the end of their school day and see what you can learn together when you engage others as bearers of God.

Contemplative Listening

There are so few moments in our lives when we feel "heard," that when someone really listens to us it can feel like a conversion experience. The therapeutic industry relies upon the fact that relationships in which people are truly listened to are quite rare.

One of the deepest spiritual experiences we can have is to be prayerfully heard. To have another person listen to you with an open heart is to feel truly welcomed. I've practiced the art of spiritual direction for many years, and I'm continually amazed at how many people are healed simply by being in the presence of someone who listens to them with a prayerful heart. I also seek to be a good listener among the young people I encounter. I want them to feel safe and free enough to tell the truth about their lives. There is something about speaking the real doubts, sufferings, and insights within us that gives a deep sense of grace and freedom.

One way to help young people experience true listening is by helping them practice contemplative listening. Contemplative listening is the practice of seeking to be fully present, open, and available to another person. It is practicing a sense of prayerful vulnerability to other people so they feel safe enough to tell their stories. Here is one way in which I help young people practice and experience prayerful listening.

Have students get into groups of three or four. I've found that adolescents often find one-on-one too intense. Explain to students that this is a process of prayerful listening in which they're invited to listen to one another as we might imagine Jesus listened when he was with people. Remind students, every time they get distracted or find themselves wandering, to just bring their attention back to the person speaking while saying gently within themselves, "God, open the ears of my heart" or "God, be with _____(name) as s/he speaks." Explain that each student will have a turn to describe an experience in which they sensed God. The primary rule of the exercise is simple: As one person shares his or her experience, the other persons in the group listen and pray silently for the speaker, with no interruptions, interjections, or gestures. Just prayerful listening—listening with an open heart.

After the groups get settled and comfortable, invite them to begin the exercise with a short prayer asking God to help them speak and listen with an awareness of God's presence in their midst. (Sometimes it's easier if you lead this prayer up front.) Then suggest a certain experience for the students to talk about. It might be an encounter this week in which they sensed God. It might be a prayer experience, or an experience of gratitude after a work day, or just a general sharing on their personal lives with God. Give them a specific topic and let them know how long each person has to talk. After you give the topic, invite them to spend a few minutes in silence gathering their thoughts. You might suggest they consider, "What is it God wants you to share?"

Now invite the students to choose one person to begin sharing while the others listen prayerfully. You may want to remind them they are not to respond or offer advice to one another; they are just to listen prayerfully. After the first speaker shares for a set time (around three to five minutes) have the listeners thank the speaker. Allow a little quiet, then have a second speaker share, and so on. (Usually, I keep time at the front of the room, but sometimes it makes sense to let groups monitor the time themselves.)

After everyone has shared, spend some time reflecting on the experience. What was it like to be listened to prayerfully? What was it like to listen in this way? How is it different from other listening experiences? How might you bring this kind of prayerful listening into daily life? Conclude with a short prayer thanking God for what has taken place.

Prayer Friends

A longer and more lasting experience of holding another person in prayer is to assign students prayer partners. You can do this during a set period such as Lent or during a camp or mission trip. The principle and practice are quite simple:

Explain that each student will be given a prayer partner. Each person is asked to pray for their partner each day in their nightly prayers before they go to sleep. In addition to this set time, students are asked to pray for their partners whenever they see or think of them throughout the day.

Choose the partners. Sometimes it's nice to do this randomly (by drawing names); other times it can be more helpful to assign student partners. After partners are assigned, have the group members spend a few minutes of silence reflecting about something they want prayer for. Have them write out these prayer requests. They can be as specific or as general as they want.

Then have the prayer partners meet and exchange these prayer requests. Give them a little time to share the requests. You also might invite students to exchange other items that will help them pray for their partners (like a small picture or personal item). I participated in one group where every student painted his or her name on a small stone. The stones were exchanged, and for three months each of us kept our partner's stone in a purse or pocket during the day and next to our bed at night as a way of keeping our partner in prayer. It can be nice to pass out candles or encourage kids to get a candle and place it in their bedrooms next to the prayer request or photos of their partners. When praying for their partners, they can light these candles to help them focus their prayers. Remind kids via email or at youth group meetings to continue praying for their partners.

At the end of the set period, bring the students to-gether to share their experiences. What was it like to hold this person in prayer for a week (a month, etc.)? Did your feelings for this person change over time? What happened to the issue that you wanted prayer for during this time? What was it like to know you were being prayed for? How did it affect your relation-ship with the person praying for you? How might you continue this kind of practice in daily life?

———ᐧᑐᐧ———

After Auri shared her story with our group in Guate-mala, I went up and spoke with her. I asked her why the students from the school persisted in visiting her and inviting her to the school, even after she'd refused them so many times. Auri looked down thoughtfully for a moment, then said, "I think it was because they were praying for me. They told me that they prayed for me each time they met, and so over time I must have entered their hearts." She smiled at me with this realization, and then added, "Once God had placed me in their hearts, they could not let go of me."

This is the hope, that by teaching kids to pray for one another, their hearts will grow bigger, mak-ing room for the neglected classmate, the irritating neighbor, and on and on until the terrorist, the corporate polluter, the violent offender, and everyone we've ever feared or demonized suddenly finds a place of hospitality within us.

14 Create

So God created the great sea monsters and every
living creature that moves, of every kind...
—GENESIS 1:21

If you look closely at a living Christian community, a person
of God, or an authentic movement within the Christian tradition, you'll soon discover some sort of creative expression,
whether it's music, architecture, poetry, liturgy, dance, painting, or other forms of sacred art. God is the Creator, the Maker. Creating is God's nature. The more transparent we are
to God, the more we find ourselves overflowing with words,
images, stories, and visions.

Every year since the age of 26, I've spent one to three
weeks on retreat. Sometimes I'm leading these retreats;
other times I'm a participant. But every time I'm on retreat,

regardless of the setting or the subject, there is one activity that will eventually take place: People will start making stuff. Whether invited or not, someone will pin a picture to a wall or make a wreath of leaves and place it on a table. A young man will sit in a lecture, drawing. An elderly woman will ask to share a poem. A retired accountant will spend the night writing in his journal, while a single mother in the next room will take out her guitar and write a song.

There is a thin space between creativity and prayer. Christian writer Madeleine L'Engle once commented that all art is religious by nature. All I know is that when people pray and seek God, it isn't long before they start writing and singing and drawing and dancing—and when people start drawing and dancing and writing and singing, it isn't long before they start sensing some other life behind all their creative impulses. As Christians we trust that creativity is an opportunity to experience intimacy with God; it's a place of vulnerability to the Holy Spirit. When we design a garden, make music, act in a local theater, or experiment with a new spaghetti sauce, we sense ourselves participating in the very creative nature of God and, therefore, draw closer to the very core of our humanity. As Matthew Fox once wrote, "'Creativity' may be the nearest one-word definition we possess for the essence of our humanity, for the true meaning of 'soul.'"[38]

[38] Matthew Fox, *Creativity: Where the Divine and the Human Meet* (Tarcher/Putnam, 2002), 26.

I've found prayer experiences that invite creativity and imagination to be quite natural and accessible to teenagers. Having recently emerged from childhood, teenagers can be quite concrete in their thinking. Their interior life is still new to them, so prayers that rely on inner thoughts or silence can sometimes be frustrating and difficult. The most accessible forms of prayer are often those in which youth have something to do with their hands, some concrete way of entering into the prayer. Prayer exercises that involve creative media such as clay, crayons, or writing can give young people ways of expressing and encountering their experiences of God while at the same time introducing them to an interior silence. Here are some of the prayer exercises I use most commonly with teenagers:

Praying with Colors

After preparing a room for prayer, I set out boxes of crayons and various sheets of drawing and construction paper. Often I borrow crayons from the Sunday school classes in our church. There is something about broken crayons with peeled wrappers that communicates a greater sense of freedom than freshly boxed Crayolas. I then explain to the youth that this is not an art exercise—they won't be required to show their pictures to anyone. (By the time they reach adolescence, many youth have received the message that drawing, music, and other forms of artistic expression are reserved for those with talent and training). I explain that this is an invitation to pray with colors. I share how sometimes word-based prayers can become repetitive and stuck or we may find it difficult to pray and don't know what to say. When we pray with colors, we're inviting God to meet us in a new way, through images and creativity.

After gathering the group in prayer and offering the time to God, I invite the young people to come forward in silence and take some paper and a handful of crayons and find places where they can pray undisturbed. After everyone finds a place to sit, I ask them to take a few moments to quietly ask God to reveal to them their prayer, just as the disciples said to Jesus, "Teach us to pray." I encourage them to not force anything, but just to let themselves draw whatever images or colors come to them in prayer. After about 20 minutes I gather them back together and invite them to share their experiences. Some kids will want to share their pictures, others won't. My focus in debriefing the prayer is to help the young people reflect on they way in which God is present to them in their prayers: "What did you notice about this kind of prayer? What was God like as you were drawing? What is it that God is seeking to bring to your attention? What is your prayer to God at this time?"

This same kind of prayer can be done with other creative media, including clay, watercolors, charcoal and paper, or finger paints. Some students will find this kind of prayer incredibly intimate and healing, while other students will find it difficult. My hope is that by the time a young person leaves my ministry they've experienced a wide variety of prayer forms and have come closer to the way in which God is seeking to pray in them.

Journaling

Journaling is a valuable spiritual practice that allows us to express our prayers in writing and gives us a place to see and reflect on our spiritual life. There have been times in my youth ministry in which I've asked students to journal at the close of a youth meeting. I've provided journals at camps and retreats, sometimes inviting youth to spend an afternoon crafting their own journals. In weekly youth group I've purchased cheap, spiral-bound notebooks for each student, keeping a box of extra notebooks for new kids. (I've found that kids feel more free to write when the journals don't look so pristine.) I make sure the students know these journals are private and kept hidden and safe between youth meetings. Some kids resist journaling at first, but over time they begin to enjoy it, as they sense that it isn't a writing assignment, but a place for silent prayer and private reflection.

Journaling can also provide a way to help kids name their experiences after engaging in more silent, interior forms of prayer. It can also be offered at the end of a day of camp or service experience as a way of reflecting prayerfully over the day. Sometimes I give people questions to meditate on, such as:

What is your prayer today?

How is God present to you?

What is God seeking to bring to your attention?

What is God's hope for you?

Regardless of how you present journaling to your group, the important thing is to let kids know that this is prayer—not a writing assignment. The intention is to be present to God through the act of writing and reflecting with words. I ask the kids to begin each journaling session by asking God to be present in their words and reflections.

Just as is the case in praying with colors, you'll find that some kids find journaling to be particularly life giving. They'll write poems or fill pages with all kinds of thoughts and ideas. Other students will find journaling frustrating and limiting. Sometimes I encourage kids who may be feeling frustrated to draw in their journals or to make lists of words that express their prayer, rather than writing sentences.

Group Creations

I once led an event in which youth groups from different communities were seeking to discern the ways in which God wanted to renew their churches. After much discussion, analysis, and brainstorming, I invited the youth to try an exercise in which each delegation of young people would pray and listen for the Spirit's leading. I had the young people from each church sit together and then gave them large sheets of butcher paper and a basket of felt pens. After spending the day talking about their churches, now it was time for them to listen and create.

We began with some silence, then prayers that we all would be open to the Spirit's leading, that we might "listen to what the Spirit is saying to the churches" (Revelation 3:22). I invited the young people to remain in prayer and silence and then together, as they felt led, to begin drawing or writing on the paper in the middle of their group. Some groups wrote words; others created whole scenes and visions of God's call to their church. Some groups had a variety of images, while others found themselves working together on a common intuited image. At the end of the exercise I had the groups look at these images and talk to one another about the experience. What had emerged in the drawing? What was God's invitation? What was missing? What was God like as they sought to do this exercise together?

Of course, these kinds of communal prayer exercises can be done using other forms of media as well. We have silently and prayerfully painted fabrics to be used for a Communion table; we have created a prayer space (while in silent prayer) using objects from nature; we have prayed with clay, forming various images that express our prayers and then, in silence, connecting these miniature sculptures in the front of our sanctuary for worship. Creating communally in prayer can sometimes be a deep experience of the way in which we are connected by the Spirit — a potent statement in a culture that seems to only value individualism.

A friend of mine has a 14-year-old daughter who is a writer. Unlike most kids her age, Elizabeth doesn't have a full calendar of activities after school. Nor does she spend her free time surfing the Internet or watching television. Most days when Elizabeth comes home from school, she lies on the couch or sits in her room daydreaming. After a while she might take the dog for a walk, draw, or flip through magazines. Following dinner she'll pick at her homework, then spend the rest of the evening hours fiddling in the kitchen or lounging around the house. Although she has friends, she isn't eager to socialize. She doesn't spend hours on the phone. But then, suddenly, usually around 10:00 at night, something happens. While her sisters and parents head off to sleep, Elizabeth will get a burst of creative energy and go intently to the family computer to begin working on her novel. With concentration and focus, she'll peer into the computer screen, typing, editing, reading, and rewriting sometimes until 1:00 or 2:00 in the morning.

Her mother worries, legitimately, about Elizabeth. She worries that Elizabeth isn't getting the right kind of sleep. She worries that Elizabeth isn't active enough and prods her to sign up for more social and physical activities. Recently, I was a guest in Elizabeth's home. I watched her pattern of lounging around the house followed by intense periods of creative concentration. I, too, worried about a young girl who is up at 1:00 a.m. Then Elizabeth showed me her writing. The work was fluid and articulate, bursting with imaginative characters. I told her father I was impressed with his daughter's writing. "Yes," he said. "I know. I'm beginning to understand that when Elizabeth is lounging around the house she's gestating. Stories are forming in her. Words and images and all these fanciful characters are growing and coming to life. She's not wasting time. She's creating."

Creativity, like prayer, requires open time. Creative expression depends upon the kind of holy leisure early Christians found so necessary to knowing God. How can kids make contact with the creativity of God if they are never given time that is sanctified and blessed, time to gestate until they sense the electricity of the Holy Spirit coalescing within them? Giving kids permission to sit and create in prayer is one of the greatest gifts we can offer them—teaching them the patience, persistence, and joy of engaging the depths of life.

Composer Leonard Bernstein described his creative process as follows: "I sit for long nights all by myself and don't have a thought in my head. I'm dry.

I'm blocked, or so it seems. I sit at the piano and just improvise—strum some chords or try a sequence of notes. And then, suddenly, I find one that hits, that suggests something else...This is the most exciting moment that can happen in an artist's life. And every time it happens...I say 'Gratias agimus tibi.' Thank you for the gift..."[39]

Like Elizabeth, young seekers of God need blessed and open time so they can gestate the life of God within them, until it spills out into colors, shapes, words, and songs—until they too are so overtaken with gratitude that they turn to the one true Maker, the Creator, saying, "Thank you. Thank you for the gift."

[39] Fox, 50.

15 Travel

They were on the road...

MARK 10:32

A few weeks after I started my first full-time youth ministry job, a parishioner bought the youth group a new 15-pas-
senger van. I received it like an answer to prayer. My youth
group, a disparate mix of kids from five different schools,
shared few interests and mostly felt like strangers to one
another. I knew the van was the key to bringing these kids
together. Soon I made sure all our meetings involved van-
related activities—such as driving scavenger hunts, trips for
ice cream, and regular rides home. When kids began arguing about which music to play, I had an auto mechanic jam
the van radio to "Sunny 910," an AM station broadcasting
hits from the 1930s, '40s, and '50s. Since I'd already banned
all earphones, video games, and other electronic entertain-

ment devices, the students in my youth group could either visit with one another or sway to the swinging sounds of Guy Lombardo, Ella Fitzgerald, and Tommy Dorsey.

"Community happens while you're doing something," my friend Frank Rogers is fond of saying. And I soon found it was van rides, more than games and mixers, that created relationships in my ministry. Soon I was taking kids on long drives in which we'd experience group bonding while singing "Mona Lisa" or "If I Knew You Were Comin' I'd've Baked a Cake." I intentionally chose retreat centers and camps that were at least half a day's travel away, knowing that five hours in the van would do more to facilitate relationships with my kids than any other activity. The conversations we had on those long drives were often more real and reflective than anything that took place once we arrived.

There's something about gathering youth together, leaving the roles and habits of our daily lives behind, and traveling in the same direction. It builds community, gives a sense of purpose, and makes us transparent to the life of God. Jesus was a traveler who often surprised his disciples by saying in the most unusual circumstances, "Let's go." How can we help young people experience times of travel as an occasion to withdraw, reflect, and draw near the One who sends us out into the world?

Moving in Silence

For most young people growing up today, travel is synonymous with entertainment. Rarely do young people travel without music, DVDs, video games, or other hand-held entertainment devices. They travel in buses with earphones blaring or in vans with video screens shimmering. Time in a car or bus is time isolated, in which kids give their attention over to some form of distraction in order to make the trip go faster.

One of the best laboratories for helping youth practice the Christian life is a church van or bus. I've found it critical to bar all electronic entertainment devices—even cell phones—from youth group trips and outings. If these items seem necessary for some reason, I still confiscate them and hold them in a safe place, and then dispense them to kids at designated times. I explain to students that the purpose of the rule isn't to create undue suffering, but to encourage people to talk to one another, to notice the landscape and surrounding environment as we travel, and to be attentive to God and the purpose of our trip.

Once I've created an "electronic-free" environment, I'll invite the young people at different points in our trip to enter into prayer and reflection. I'll pull over and give kids instructions to refrain from conversation and look out the windows at the surroundings (whether urban or rural), asking God to help them see as God sees. How is God present in this place?

Sometimes I'll give kids a question to meditate on as we travel. I'll ask them, "What is God's hope for you on this trip?" or "What is your prayer on this event?" Then I'll invite the youth to spend anywhere from 10 to 30 minutes in silence. Afterward, we'll talk about what they noticed in the prayer.

Of course, there are times when the youth are so excited on a trip that silent prayer is simply not possible. Try to pay attention to when the chatter and energy slows and the group is becoming more reflective. There are moments on long trips when kids will become quiet and move inward. Prayer is more accessible when youth are already feeling reflective, safe, and attentive to their surroundings.

Walking Prayer

One of the central activities in Jesus' ministry on earth was walking. Jesus walked...a lot. Most of the time he walked with friends and seekers. I find that walking forms of prayer help us sense God not only in the quiet, but also in the sights, sounds, and movement of our own bodies. Jesus sent the disciples out to walk among towns and villages; he sent them to go out on foot and carry the gospel. Walking in prayer can be a similar experience of our holding the good news of Jesus. Walking slows us down to God's speed; walking in prayer gives way to strolling, meandering, and enjoying ourselves with God. Here's an exercise that invites young people to walk with Jesus, just as the disciples did years ago.

Begin by explaining that followers of Jesus often traveled with him—asking questions, listening to his teaching, and noticing the birds, flowers, trees, and other natural objects Jesus would point to as signs and symbols of God's love. Tell kids that in this form of prayer we're seeking to share a similar experience of walking and listening to Jesus.

If your prayer involves walking to a particular destination, make sure students know the route. Ask the youth to keep space between themselves to allow each person room enough to give their full attention to Jesus. If there is no particular destination, make sure you give students the physical boundaries for the exercise so they don't get lost and can hear you when you call them back.

Once the instructions and boundaries are set, invite kids to take a walk with Jesus. Ask them to spend a few minutes in silence and prayer, offering this time to God. Then, when they're ready, say in prayer, "Jesus, walk with me." Encourage them to pay special attention to what they see and hear and feel as they walk. If there are words that come to them, encourage them to share these with Jesus, just as they would if they were walking with a friend. Let them know there may be times when they're just walking, enjoying the presence of Jesus without having any particular words or insights. Tell students that anytime they get distracted or lost in thought and forget they're praying, they can simply say, "Jesus, walk with me," and bring their attention back to the presence of Jesus.

When the prayer is over or the destination reached, gather the students together and ask them to share their experiences. What did they notice? What was Jesus like? How was this different from other times of walking?

This past summer I attended England's Christian festival called Greenbelt. Each night of the festival, organizers held a prayer vigil for climate change. Most people gathered for these prayer services were under 30. These vigils sought to direct the prayers and actions of Christians on behalf of the earth and the poor who suffer most from the effects of drought and high temperatures. While images of empty lake beds, brown crops, melting ice caps, and hungry people were displayed, we lit candles and prayed that we in the Western world would repent from consumptive activities that bring great suffering and destruction to God's planet and people. We prayed that God would give us the courage and inspiration to heal the earth, to turn from modes of transportation and production that bring suffering and destruction.

In 2007 more than 2,500 scientists from around the globe gathered for a United Nations summit on global warming. The report they issued is bleak, offering what the scientist' called a "near-apocalyptic" vision of the state of the earth: More than a billion people in need of water, extreme food shortages in Africa, the earth's landscape ravaged by floods, and millions of species sentenced to extinction. Scientists put the blame for the impending crisis on the culture, lifestyle, and consumptive practices of the industrial nations (that's us).

It seems time that Christian youth workers and young people reflect prayerfully concerning our transportation habits. How might churches and youth groups reduce carbon emissions due to travel? I love church vans, but what if we biked to camp—praying and singing as we pedaled? What if we took public transportation to the mission field? What if we asked youth to walk to church as a weekly pilgrimage? What if we sought to create a "zero-emissions" ministry?

As Christians, we're asked to "walk in God's ways." Might we be more transparent to God's love when we tread lightly on the earth? As we integrate prayer and travel I believe the Holy Spirit will continue to challenge Christians to reflect, repent, and then create simple forms of travel that reflect God's way of life.

16 Reflect

I think of you on my bed, and meditate on you in the watches of the night.

—PSALM 63:6

It was during my junior high years at Yosemite Sierra Summer Camp that I experienced a powerful influence on my formation as a Christian. Created by a veteran youth leader and staffed with students from Christian colleges and seminaries (many of them youth ministry students), the camp had all the elements needed to awaken longing in a young person's heart. This was classic summer camp—with tree-soaked air, heartfelt singing, firelight stories, summer romances, lakeside sunsets, quiet-time confessions, and the electricity of new friendships. Yet unlike other camps that featured a weeklong buildup to an altar call, this camp lasted three full weeks, thus offering us a simple experience of Christian living.

The three-week length dissipated the novelty and exoticism of camp life. It made it more difficult for staff to maintain high-energy facades, allowing ordinary relationships to develop between kids and staff. Unlike other camps that often felt like high-energy revivals, this camp offered a slow retreat that gently immersed us in practices that invited spiritual reflection and an embodied awareness of what life in Christ felt like. The structure of our camp days revolved around a rhythm of morning devotions and evening worship, not unlike a monastic community. Because of the three-week span, the schedule was slow and uncluttered with activities. Conversations and relationships weren't forced but were allowed to happen naturally.

Each summer students were clustered in small groups of the same age and sex, and each group was assigned an adult counselor to befriend and guide us during our stay. For three weeks our counselor was our companion at every meal, recreational event, and worship gathering. He slept in our cabin, led evening devotions, answered our late-night questions, and pastored us through our different moods and difficulties.

This intensive relationship invited me into the life of an adult Christian in a way I'd never experienced outside of my family. I remember listening as our counselor, Marcello, talked about his hopes of marriage. I remember him coming to our cabin depressed and dejected after an angry phone conversation with his father. I remember staying up late night after night listening to him patiently answering our questions about sex, faith, and other mysteries of adult life. And I still recall the stories he shared about his first job, a friendship that went bad, and the difficulty of immigrating to the United States from Argentina. Through his stories and openness Marcello revealed to us what Christian adulthood could be like.

I remember the last night of my final summer at camp. After ice-cream sundaes and counselor skits, Marcello brought us back to our cabin and with a somber face told us to dress warmly for a walk out to the woods. We dressed quietly, somehow sensing the need for a ritual on this final night. It was near 1:00 a.m. as we lined up outside our cabin, watching our breath rise like incense against the starlit night. Marcello came out, slowly looked at all of us, and then turned and headed for the trees. With no need for instruction, we followed. The camp was dark and shadowy, silent apart from the crunch of our shoes shuffling on the graveled pathway. As we came to the edge of the forest, he stopped and asked us to sit on the pine-needled ground. I sat still and attentive, looking up at him, soaking in the import of this last night. In sparse sentences he told us we were leaving childhood. We were on our way to becoming adults. We would no longer be allowed to return to this camp. On this night it was important that each of us pray and reflect on his future. What were our gifts? What were our weaknesses? Who was God calling us to be? We were directed to stay at the edge of the forest and spend some time in prayerful reflection. He told us to try to see ourselves the way God sees us, then ask God to give us an image of the man God longed for each of us to be. Marcello looked reflectively at each of us, and then walked into a clearing about 50 yards away and sat on the largest stone among a cluster of boulders. I looked at my cabinmates. Instead of the smirks and squirreliness that afflicted most of our gatherings, I saw them sitting with bowed heads earnestly obeying our guide's direction.

I too lowered my head in my hands and, with eyes clenched tight, began to pray. I tried to see myself through God's eyes. I immediately felt ashamed for the ways in which I treated my brother and could feel the way my teasing hurt him. I thought of the other kids at camp and felt remorse about the kids I'd made fun of, using them as a source of humor. I then had an image of myself at that moment, sitting in the woods praying. I could feel God's compassion at the pain I was feeling over my parents' divorce. I sat, receiving this compassion, and then asked God to show me who I would become—who it was that God was forming me into. I remember praying that God would help me to be like Jesus.

Then Marcello began to call our names, one by one. I watched as each cabinmate rose and walked ceremoniously toward our elder. I noticed how Marcello looked at each boy, gently smiling, greeting each one with an embrace. I watched as each of my friends sat on one of the smaller stones. I stared as he spoke to them in a low whisper. Forgetting my prayer, I wondered what words he was imparting, what he would say to me. Each time he finished speaking to a boy, Marcello returned to silent prayer until he called the next boy. I waited as he called one after another, until I was the only one left at the forest's edge.

Finally he called my name. I felt awkward and self-conscious as I tried to walk unhurriedly to where he stood. I felt relieved as I looked at his warm and welcoming face. I sat next to him, and he asked what had come to me in prayer. I confessed the mean and often hurtful teasing I did to my brother and to others at camp. I talked about the pain of my parents' divorce and my realization that God also felt this pain. I talked about Jesus as a brave person, and that I too hoped to be brave. Marcello listened intently, and then in an intimate and intentional manner, he began to describe all the gifts he saw in me, all the moments when he'd sensed God alive in me. In prophetic phrasing, he began to tell me all the ways in which he saw me growing into manhood and all the attributes I was developing that would bring light to others. He then laid his hand on my head and prayed in simple words. He prayed for healing and forgiveness for the hurt I'd caused others and then thanked God for me, asking that I might become the man he saw me becoming.

That was the first time I remember being invited to stop and reflect prayerfully on my own life. Although it was nearly 30 years ago, the power of that self-examination is still with me today. I never saw Marcello after that 1979 summer camp, but I have clung to his words of forgiveness and blessing as if they were the words of a prophet. I have measured my life by them and stretched to live up to them. His words were the assurance that God was at work in me, a God who would lead and guide me into a full and abundant life.

All prayer is an invitation to self-reflection. We turn our attention to God, and in the light of God's love we notice faults and blemishes; we awaken displaced desires; we reconnect with repressed dreams and feel the pull of our strengths and gifts. Helping young people examine their lives in prayer isn't a psychological exercise. It's deeper than that. Prayerful self-reflection invites repentance, a turning from our own self-preoccupation to allow God to convict, heal, and inspire us toward the person God created us to be. In a world full of distractions, times of prayerful reflection and self-examination can help keep young people from being swayed by the pull of the culture, so they might stay close to their own calling and vocation.

Confessing Our Brokenness

I have a small office in the basement of our church. Every day at noon people gather in a nearby room and confess their lives. These groups of broken and transparent people are hosted by Alcoholics Anonymous.

I'm always surprised at the people who show up to these meetings—successful business leaders, college students, sporty moms, community activists, and even friends in ministry. Many of these people attend our church. At a recent Sunday service a member of one of these groups told her story. She shared that it was the "confessing" nature of AA that helped her stay truthful about her destructive habits and remember "the goodness" that was in her. Her words reminded me of the importance of step 4 in the 12-step program, which invites people to make a "fearless inventory" of themselves.

In this exercise, young people are given the opportunity to examine their own lives—their behaviors, attitudes, personality traits, and actions—in order to gain a deeper awareness of the ways in which their lives are distorted, out of sync with the good that God seeks to grow in them.

Begin by preparing a space for prayer and handing out journals and pens. Explain to students that together you're going to practice a prayer of confession. Confession allows us to examine the ways we are moving away from or impeding the life God wants for us. Paul reminds us that, "All have sinned and fall (Romans 3:23) short of the glory of God." It's important for young people to recognize that sin is a human condition—a condition in which we turn our backs on God's grace, refusing to be hospitable and grateful to God, and friendly and compassionate toward others. Since the beginning of the Christian faith, believers have found it helpful and necessary to confess to God the ways in which they are weak and hurtful, so they can repair any damage they may have inflicted on others or themselves and renew their love and commitment to Jesus' way of love.

Have students examine prayerfully their behaviors over the preceding day or week. Invite them to ask Jesus in prayer, "What are my sins?" Sometimes it might be helpful to give students a list that helps them examine their behavior. This list might include things like selfishness, dishonesty, resentment, jealousy, greed, envy, hatred, unkindness, pride, judgmentalism, impatience, and lack of faith. Have students confess their sins on paper either by writing a list or maybe even a letter to God describing these sins. Let students know their confessions will remain private.

Have students gather in small groups and share what it was like to notice these sins. What is God's invitation to them?

It's important to close this time of confession with a ritual or prayer that reminds young people of God's love that inspires us to let go of our destructive ways and return to God's way of life. If confessions are written, I sometimes collect them, offer a prayer of forgiveness, and then burn them. Other times I simply tear them up as a sign of God's forgiveness and love—and then offer a prayer of pardon and blessing over the young people.

Confessing Our Gifts

It can also be helpful to do an exercise similar to the one above, but have the students "confess" their gifts—the moments when they were living within the spirit of God's grace and love. Have the students review their behavior over the previous day or week, except this time have them list or write out moments when they were living in ways that reflect God's love. You might even make a list that might help them recognize the fruits of the Spirit and other signs of God's presence in their lives. This list might include patience, kindness, encouragement, acceptance, humility, love, joy, generosity, honesty, peace, self-control, service, self-sacrifice, and gentleness. Have students write down moments when they were living in the spirit of Jesus and then share these moments in small groups. What do they notice about themselves as they reflect on these moments in prayer? Have the group gather in prayer and give thanks to God for the ways in which these young people reveal God's love in their lives.

Awareness Examen

The awareness examen helps us trace God's presence and call within our exterior and interior life experience. Nearly five centuries ago, Ignatius of Loyola, founder of the Jesuit order, wrote *The Spiritual Exercises*—a collection of prayer methods that have been used by retreatants for centuries. Of all the practices and exercises Ignatius employed, he felt the *examen* (which means "examination") was the most essential. I've used this prayer consistently with youth and youth ministry teams and found it to be particularly powerful in helping individuals and groups stay close to the Spirit of God.[40]

This prayer invites young people to identify moments of consolation and desolation. *Consolation* is a classical term used over the centuries by praying Christians to identify moments when we are more open to God, ourselves, and others. These are moments of connection, moments when we feel more alive, more transparent to God, and more loving toward other people. *Desolation* refers to the opposite experience—times of disconnection, depletion, alienation, and a sense of being blocked to the presence of God, others, or ourselves. By paying attention to the moments of consolation and desolation in our lives, we become more aware of the revelatory nature of our experiences. Sometimes we notice patterns or occasions when we are in the flow of God's love; other times we see moments when we seem to be caught up in our own wounds and blindness.

After you've prepared the room for prayer, explain the steps of the prayer to the students. You may want to hand out pens or journals.

Invite the group to get comfortable and ready for prayer and then lead them in a centering exercise to help them draw their awareness toward God (see chapter 4). Then ask the young people to invite the Holy Spirit (or Jesus) to accompany them as they go over the experiences of the day— from when they first woke up to this moment right now. As they go through their day in prayer, encourage them to allow this question to arise: "For what moment was I most grateful?" Allow little things to emerge: A smile from a stranger,

[40] To learn how I've used this prayer within youth ministry teams and programs, see *Contemplative Youth Ministry* (Zondervan, 2006).

the sunlight through a window, a kind act from a teacher, an engaging conversation. Choose one of these moments to meditate on. What does it have to teach you about your life with God? Don't force anything—just be open and let the moment arise that seems to hold the most gratitude. You may want to invite students to journal their responses to this exercise.

After some time, ask students to go back over their day in prayer, this time reflecting on a different question: "For what moment was I least grateful?" Instruct students to allow God to bring their attention to whatever moment seemed most filled with desolation—disconnection, alienation, an absence of God's Spirit. Again, give students a few moments to prayerfully consider or journal their prayer.

Finally, call students together and have them share their experiences from the prayer. In light of their reflections, what is God's call to them?

I've engaged youth in this prayer at youth group meetings, after long days on mission trips, and at retreat settings. One time during the 40 days of Lent, we had each young person in our youth group pair up with an adult and do this prayer over the phone each night before bed. We noticed over time that our behaviors and relationships shifted as we became more conscious of the way in which God's Spirit was calling us to live.

Sometimes it's helpful to vary the questions used in the examen. Other questions you might use for this prayer include: When did I give and receive the most love? When did I give and receive the least love? When did I feel most alive? When did I feel least alive? When did I feel most free? When did I feel least free?[41]

Meditation on the Words of Jesus

Many of the questions Jesus asks in the Scriptures can cut to the heart.

I've created a list of questions Jesus speaks in the New Testament. I sometimes choose a question for the youth and then send them all out to pray that question; other times I let them see the list of questions I've compiled and choose the one that seems most relevant to them. Once the youth have a question, I'll send them out with paper and pen to pray. I ask them to take a moment in silence to offer themselves to God, and then read the question as if Jesus were asking them this question right now, today. I then ask them to respond to the question on paper. When they finish

---

[41] These questions come from *Sleeping with Bread*, by Dennis Linn, Sheila Fabricant Linn and Matthew Linn (Paulist Press, 1995).

writing, I ask them to read the question again and see if something different shows up. I encourage them to keep reading the question and responding until they feel they've received all they can from this word of God. Here is just a sampling of questions I use:

- Why do you see the speck in your neighbor's eye, but do not notice the log in your own eye? (Matthew 7:3)

- Why are you afraid? (Matthew 8:26)

- Why did you doubt? (Matthew 14:31)

- Are your hearts hardened? (Mark 8:17)

- Do you have eyes, and fail to see? Do you have ears, and fail to hear? (Mark 8:18)

- Who do you say that I am? (Mark 8:29)

- Why do you call me "Lord, Lord," and do not do what I tell you? (Luke 6:46)

- Where is your faith? (Luke 8:25)

- What does it profit you if you gain the whole world, but lose yourself? (Luke 9:25)

- Can any of you by worrying add a single hour to your span of life? (Luke 12:25)

- What is the kingdom of God like? (Luke 13:18)

- What do you want me to do for you? (Luke 18:41)

- What are you looking for? (John 1:38)

- Do you want to be made well? (John 5:6)

- Do you love me more than these? (John 21:15)

In a similar way, you can invite students to practice self-examination and confession in light of the Beatitudes, as is commonly done within the Orthodox tradition. Hand out a copy of the Beatitudes. (I like to use Eugene Peterson's interpretation from *The Message*.[42]) Invite students to read them and reflect on their own lives in light of Jesus' words. Encourage them to reflect on the following questions: What confessions come to mind in response to the Beatitudes? What graces or gratitudes come to mind? What prayer fills your heart as you reflect on your life in light of the Beatitudes?

Necessary to any experience of self-examination is an abiding sense that God loves us. Without an awareness of God's love, our reflections can be unduly critical and even harmful. Most of us carry an "inner voice of shame" that constantly reminds us of our shortcomings and faults. A Western culture that values the rich and beautiful only confirms this interior voice. It's important to remember the counsel of author and spiritual director Marjorie Thompson: "Self examination and confession do not call us to self-hatred or self-condemnation; they open the door of our heart to cleansing, renewal, and peace."[43] Young people need the constant reminder of God's love in order to enter into prayers that invite self-reflection.

Similarly, it is also important for young people to have an understanding of sin and the separation and brokenness that inhabit both human beings and the systems and structures in which we live. Self-examination done without an understanding of the need for human repentance can become sentimental and self-absorbed. Christian Smith's extensive research on the spiritual life of teenagers concluded that, in the view of most teenage Christians, "God is not demanding...his job is to solve our problems and make people feel good. In short, God is something like a combination of Divine Butler and Cosmic Therapist."[44] Jesus calls us to a relationship with the living God that can turn us away from our self-preoccupation and toward lives of love and self-sacrifice. Young people can hear this call within their own life experience as they hold up their lives to the light of God's truth.

[43] *Soul Feast* (Westminster John Knox, 1995), 84.

[44] Christian Smith with Melinda Lundquist Denton, *Soul Searching: The Religious and Spiritual Lives of American Teenagers*, (Oxford, 2005), 165.

17 Suffer

Lord, have mercy…

MATTHEW 20:30

Adolescence is a birthing process. As we move from childhood to adulthood, there is a dawning awareness of the pleasures of friendship, romance, and sexuality—all of these accompany expanding physical, emotional, and intellectual capacities. But author and pastor Frederick Buechner suggests that the most powerful awareness that's experienced in adolescence is suffering. "What do I do with this pain?" students ask. "How do I live with suffering?" Buechner writes:

> *Let me suggest with total inaccuracy that the word adolescent is made up of the Latin preposition* ad, *meaning*

"toward," and the Latin noun dolor, *meaning "pain." Thus "adolescent" becomes a term that designates human beings who are in above all else a painful process, more specifically those who are in the process of discovering pain itself, of trying somehow to come to terms with pain, to figure out how to deal with pain, not just how to survive pain but how to turn it to some human and creative use in their own encounters with it.*[45]

What do we do with mindless, illogical, unstoppable, unfixable suffering? This is the big question that awakens in adolescence. The world is a cruel place. Innocent people suffer without cause—storms rise out of the ocean and drown the good and evil alike; cells mutate and cause cherub-faced children to deteriorate and die; earthquakes bury whole communities while they sleep.

Suffering draws a person's soul to the surface. It brings some people to God and turns others away from God. Suffering is where faith becomes real or disappears like a childhood daydream. Adolescence is a time of reflecting on suffering. (Author and psychoanalyst Erik Erikson found that it is only the

[45] *Secrets in the Dark: A Life in Sermons* (Harper San Francisco, 2006), 207.

young and the old who meditate on death.) It's suffering that often awakens the adolescent soul. It's suffering in particular that causes young people, from even the most agnostic of families, to stay awake at night pleading with God for comfort and healing.

We make space for young people to pray because in the midst of suffering there is a persistent invitation to cry out, to appeal for justice and ask for mercy. Many of the prayers and psalms of the Bible give voice to suffering:

How long, O Lord? Will you forget me for ever?...
How long must I bear pain in my soul, and have
sorrow in my heart all day long? (PSALM 13:1, 2)

Turn to me and be gracious to me, for I am lonely
and afflicted. Relieve the troubles of my heart, and
bring me out of my distress. (PSALM 25:16-17)

Give ear to my prayer...My heart is in anguish within
me, the terrors of death have fallen upon me. (PSALM
55:1, 4)

Hear my prayer, O Lord; let my cry come to you...

For I eat ashes like bread, and mingle tears with

my drink. (PSALM 102:1, 9)

These prayers from the Psalms could easily be pulled from the journals of many teenagers. Sadly, most teenagers are trained by churches to keep the agony and pain of their lives a secret. They see the way we dress up for church, they watch as we greet one another with serene and pleasant faces, they note the neat and orderly way in which we worship, and they conclude that church is a place of pretending, a place for hiding all the mess and anguish of human living.

Prayer is one way in which we help young people endure and transform suffering. Prayer allows us to penetrate the fear and pain we experience in this life and make contact with the God who holds the burden of living.

Mother Teresa, a woman who knew suffering intimately within her own life as well as among the sick and dying of India, once commented, "Suffering in and of itself is useless, but suffering that is shared with the passion of Christ is a wonderful gift and a sign of love. Suffering, pain, sorrow, humiliation, feelings of loneliness, are nothing but the kiss of Jesus, a sign that you have come so close that He can kiss you."[46] We help kids pray into their suffering and the suffering of the world so they too might feel the kiss of Jesus in the midst of the misery and pain of living.

Images of Suffering

In the Western world we live within a constant stream of sounds and images that immerse us in the tragedy and violence of the world. We grow so familiar with the sight of grieving mothers, war-torn countries, and hungry children that it's easy for our hearts to grow numb. As I write these words, the United States is entering its fifth year of occupation and war in Iraq. My morning newspaper reports that 18 Iraqi civilians were killed yesterday by American forces. The gas tank of a car carrying a young Iraqi couple and their child caught fire after being riddled with gunshots. When medics retrieved the bodies, they found the mother and infant were so badly charred that their bodies had fused together. We've heard so many stories of suffering and pain in Iraq over the past five years that many of us have become anesthetized—no longer capable of feeling the horror, pain, and suffering the Iraqi people and American soldiers are experiencing.

[46] Becky Benenate and Joseph Durepos ed., *No Greater Love* (MJF Books, 1997), 137. Mother Teresa suffered incredible interior anguish throughout most of her adult life. Read her letters and correspondence with her various spiritual directors and supervisors in *Mother Teresa: Come Be My Light* (Doubleday 2007).

As Christians we seek to believe that Christ is particularly present within those who are powerless, hopeless, and hurting. One of the central tasks in discipling young people is to help them seek out God's love and hope in the midst of harsh and destructive places. The Christian faith is undercut if young people are trained to see God only in the bright and loving places of the world. Jesus' life and ministry are powerful because of the way in which Jesus revealed the intimacy and companionship of God within the depths of human suffering.

Opening our hearts and expanding the love of God within the world's and our own personal suffering has to begin by being present to the suffering. We seek God's light in the darkness by first entering into the darkness. Just as Jesus looked at and listened to lepers, grieving widows, lame and wounded people, so too are we called to bear witness to the misery that is present in the world. It is in taking a long, loving look at the real agony of the world that we uncover God's compassion and companionship.

One prayer exercise that invites youth to allow the "scales to fall from their eyes" and really see and feel the suffering in our world is a prayer that involves gazing and praying with images. After preparing the room and explaining the steps of the prayer, pass out pictures from newspapers and Web sites that contain images of suffering. Depending on the picture, it might be helpful to include the accompanying story or caption for the picture.

Invite youth to find a place in the room where they can pray with their image. Encourage them to begin the prayer by asking God to open their eyes and hearts to the suffering of others. When they're ready, invite the youth to spend a few moments just gazing prayerfully at the image. What's happening in the picture? What are the various people experiencing? How would you respond if you were present when this photo was taken? How do you feel now?

After exploring this picture ask Jesus, "How were you present in this experience?" Spend a few moments reflecting on Jesus' presence in silence. Then ask, "Jesus, what is your call to me as I look on these people?" You might want to have journals available for youth to write down their responses.

Gather the group together and share their responses. Then ask the youth, "What do you imagine is the prayer of the people in your photo?" After taking a moment to hear their prayers, invite the group to close by having each person pray the prayer that he or she imagines is being prayed by the people in the picture.

Prayer around the Cross

The cross is not only a symbol of the suffering Christ endured but also a living reminder of the continual suffering Christ endures through the lives of the afflicted among us. Many Catholics meditate frequently on images of the suffering Christ that are found on crucifixes hanging within their parishes and homes. Most Protestants prefer the empty cross as a sign of Christ's resurrection; yet the cross remains a powerful reminder of human cruelty, sin, and suffering.

In prayer services held by the brothers in Taizé, France, there is a particular moment in which an icon of the crucified Jesus painted upon a cross is laid upon the floor. People are then invited to come and pray around the cross. I've attended many Taizé prayer services and have found this time of praying around the cross to be very profound, as it invites people to bring their own suffering, the world's sufferings, and the suffering of Jesus together in prayer.[47]

The following prayer service is one example of how you might invite young people to pray and sense the suffering of God within their own lives and communities. This service can be used as a Good Friday

[47] To learn more see www.taize.fr/en.

service and is particularly powerful when it is held with an intergenerational community. Like Taizé prayer, the prayer occurs primarily through song.

Quietly gather. The space should invite prayer and silent reflection as people quietly enter. A large cross should be stood at the front of the room; candles and sacred images can be used to create a prayerful atmosphere.

Singing. Once people have gathered, the song leader begins to sing. This singing is in the tradition of Christian chant—it is singing as prayer. Songs are simple, often one or two lines from Scripture that are sung continuously. This style of singing/chanting frees one from concentrating on words or melody, allowing a person to drop into prayer. The repetitive nature of the singing keeps the mind busy enough so the heart's attention can deepen and draw toward the Presence of the Holy. Participants are encouraged to sing but also may enjoy just listening, allowing the music to wash over them. It's important that the leader understand this song-leading as prayer rather than performance.[48]

Word. Read a Scripture passage about Jesus' suffering on the cross or the suffering people who came to Jesus (such as Luke 18:35-43 or Luke 23:26-49). Alternately, you might choose to read a psalm of suffering (such as Psalm 22, 42, or 82). Read the passage twice, the second time a bit slower than the first. In this way people are encouraged to pray into the passage, much like *lectio divina*.

Cross. After a few minutes of silence, have two people take the cross and lay it on the floor. Make sure there is plenty of room for people to come and kneel around the cross. Invite the young people to spend a few minutes of silence (or with music playing) reflecting on the suffering they carry in their own lives or the suffering they carry for others—family, friends, the earth, situations in the world.

Singing. As the group is led in singing, invite those who feel called to come forward and pray around the cross. This is a time for young people to bring their prayers to Jesus. Place unlit votive candles around the cross and allow people to light a candle as a symbol of their prayer. Let the singing continue as a way of holding the prayers of those who are coming forward as well as those who remain seated.

Spoken prayers. When the students have finished praying and returned to their seats, invite them to speak their prayers aloud. The leader of the service asks for prayers of petition, and then time is allowed for people to speak a prayer out loud. Each person closes his or her prayer with "God, in your grace," and the community responds, "Hear our prayer."

The Lord's Prayer. At the close of spoken prayers, the leader invites the group to pray the Lord's Prayer.

Singing. The song leader then leads the group in a final chant.

Quietly depart. The leader offers one line of closing or sending out and ends with "Amen."

This prayer service typically lasts anywhere from 45 to 75 minutes, depending on the number of people and the length of singing. Prayer around the cross doesn't have to be restricted to a prayer service—there may be other occasions when you might feel drawn to place a cross on the floor and have students pray around it, lighting candles as a symbol of their prayers to the One who knows our pain.

Present to the Pain

Praying for others can be abstract when we only imagine them in our minds. Our prayer is more real and rich when we can actually see, hear, and feel the suffering we seek to pray for. Instead of praying for the sick from your youth room, take students to a hospital where they can sit in the waiting room and see the worried families or stand outside the children's ward and see the children lying in bed. Instead of praying for the poor from your church sanctuary, take young people to shelters, food banks, and parts of your community where the poor live. Send them out to walk and pray within these places—pray for the people they see and hear.

I once took a group of high school students out to fields filled with migrant workers who spent their days bent over, harvesting fruit. The youth watched the back-breaking work these people did to provide food for others. We then went and prayed among the rundown and crowded apartments where these workers lived. After sitting, feeling, watching, and praying for these people, one young woman in our youth group asked if we might throw a Christmas party for the workers. Three months later we rented a community hall near the fields and hosted a party for farm workers and their families. We had music, crafts, cookie-making, and games for the children. At the end of the evening, youth group members gave the children Christmas presents they had purchased and wrapped themselves. A community activist later told me these presents were probably the only Christmas presents some of the children would receive. By taking youth out of the youth room and into the lives of suffering people, not only were their hearts opened to the needs of others, they were also inspired to engage in creative acts of love.

———⟿———

I remember a very bright and committed young woman in my youth group who struggled with an eating disorder. Eventually her condition became so disabling that she was hospitalized. One day I went to visit her in the hospital. Like many young women who battle with anorexia, Diane was highly accomplished. She was an "A" student, an athlete, and the leader of many school clubs. She loved to spend her weekends working in various community service groups and was strongly committed to her church and her faith. Until she was hospitalized, she'd managed to keep her eating disorder a secret.

When I went to see her in the hospital, Diane was friendly toward me but clearly was ashamed to be there. We made small talk for a while and then fell into a long, awkward silence. At a loss as to what to say, I asked if I could pray for her. Knowing she was a committed Christian, I asked how she was praying during this time. She told me she liked to pray with the Bible. I took out my Bible and asked if there were a particular verse I could read and pray with. Without hesitation she said, "Psalm 22." Tears came to my eyes as I realized that the words of despair that Jesus turned to on the cross were the best expression of what this beautiful, capable, successful young woman was feeling.

I pulled a chair up to the bedside and read Psalm 22 as Diane lay with eyes closed. My tears fell on the pages as I came across verses like: "My God, my God, why have you forsaken me? Why are you so far from helping me?...O my God, I cry by day, but you do not answer; and by night, but find no rest; I am poured out like water...my hands and feet have shriveled; I can count all my bones ... O Lord, do not be far away! O my help, come quickly to my aid!" (vv. 1, 2, 14, 16-17, 19)

No one suspected this prayer resided in Diane, least of all me; and yet this was her secret prayer. At that time in my ministry, the youth group I led was easygoing with lots of fun and laughter. There had been little room for Diane, or other youth, to allow the real suffering of their hearts to be heard. Yet it was within Diane's suffering that God called her to prayer. As I left the hospital that day I made a commitment to make space in my ministry for the suffering of young people.

Young people need prayer because they are just as broken as the rest of humanity. They need prayer in order to learn how to surrender, how to give up control, how to ask for help, how to turn their lives over to the deeper reality of God's love. Prayer, particularly in adolescence, grows out of suffering. Youth ministry is simply a babysitting service if it doesn't help young people come home to the suffering they experience in the world.

18 Heal

Moved with pity, Jesus stretched out his hand and
touched him…
—MARK 1:41

One of my spiritual mentors, author and Episcopal priest
Morton Kelsey, used to lead retreats that often included
a healing service. Based on his many years of experience,
he knew that many in the group would be skeptical about
healing. Weren't healing services for televangelists? Could
thinking, reasonable Christians really expect God to heal? In
response to these questions Morton would pick up a special
Bible from which he had carefully cut out every passage that
referred to Jesus healing people. He would hold up the Bible
and slowly flip through the Gospels, each page filled with
holes, and say, "You can't trust the words of Jesus without

trusting his worldview. You can't hold up his acts of justice without holding up his acts of healing."

Every human being longs for healing—the crippled child, the bitter spouse, the depressed teenager. It is the Spirit of God within us that longs for wholeness, completeness, health, and vitality. In response to these hurts and needs, Jesus says, "Come." In the Gospels we find that Jesus is welcoming, unafraid, and compassionate toward everyone who comes to him in need. Those who sought healing from Jesus departed with a greater sense of well-being, wholeness, clarity, joy, health, and liveliness.

What takes place when someone is healed? I don't know. Why are some people healed while others continue to suffer? I don't know. What can we do to get the Holy Spirit to heal people? Nothing—we don't control the Holy Spirit.

So why do we invite young people to seek healing from God? We seek healing from God because Jesus was a healer. We seek healing because we believe and know the Spirit of Jesus is alive today seeking to comfort and heal those who suffer. We invite young people to seek healing because, as emulators of Jesus, we too welcome the broken among us and hold them up in prayer, so they might find peace and well-being in God.

Carried to Jesus

Here's an imaginative form of prayer that invites greater awareness of the places within us that wait for healing:

- After preparing a space, tell the story of Jesus' healing of the paralytic in Mark 2:1-12. Tell the kids this prayer will be an invitation for each of them to allow their hurt and pain to be carried to Jesus for healing. Then explain the steps of the prayer.

- Begin with a centering exercise: *Imagine your-self in the presence of God's love, surrounding and holding you like warm sunlight. Notice your breathing, without altering it. Just imagine you are breathing in God's light and love.* (Pause for a few moments.)

- *Let your awareness move down into the core of your body. See if you can feel or sense a hurt for which you still need healing. Perhaps there's anger, fear, a sense of shame, or some other pain.*

- *How does this hurt live inside your body? Perhaps you feel an ache in your chest, a lump in your throat, a knot in your stomach, a pain in your forehead. Spend a few moments simply noticing this place that is in need of healing. Approach it with care and gentleness, as if you were approaching a hurt pet or child. If this part of you could speak, what might it say to you? Spend a few minutes listening to the words and feelings from this place of hurt. What does this place of hurt want to say to you?*

- *Now imagine a group of people who love you—friends or family members, a pastor or teacher. Imagine that these people came to you just like the people who came to their paralyzed friend. (Pause for a few moments.) Now imagine that these people who love you lifted you up on a stretcher and carried you to Jesus. What do you feel, what do you hear, what do you see as you're being carried to Jesus?*

- *Imagine that your friends carry you through a crowd and into a small home and finally lay you at the feet of Jesus. You look up and see that Jesus is looking at you. What is it like to feel Jesus looking at you with compassion? (Pause.)*

- *Now imagine that Jesus reaches out and places his hand on you...maybe it's on the place in you that's in need of healing, maybe it's on your forehead or heart. For a few moments just allow Jesus to touch and pray for this place in you that is in need of healing.*

- *Now notice what you're feeling in your body. What is it like to have Jesus pray and care for this place in you? What are you like as you receive Jesus' love and compassion? Are there any insights, ideas, or actions that come to you as you receive Jesus' love and care?*

- *Imagine Jesus helps you up from the floor. You turn and thank your friends, and then turn and thank*

Jesus for his prayer. Jesus invites you to come back to him any time to pray further about this place of hurt. You offer thanks to Jesus and then turn and walk outside. (Pause for a few moments.)

- *Now take a few moments to offer thanks to God for whatever has occurred within your prayer, and then gently bring your attention back to this room.*

- Gather students together and ask them to share. Let them know they don't have to share the specifics of the prayer, and they can share as much or as little as they feel comfortable with.

- Close the group by praying that God's healing might take place for those in need.

Healing Service

Healing services offer opportunities for youth and adults to bring their pain and suffering to God for prayer. Healing was a central part of Jesus' ministry; and youth ministry is in many ways a ministry of healing. I've used the following service at youth events and youth pastor retreats as well as in various other church settings. For this service, it's necessary to have safe, trustworthy people who are able to pray for others.

Preparation. It's helpful to hold this service in a sacred space like a sanctuary or chapel. If this isn't possible, then prepare a space to be intimate and open to the Holy Spirit and prayer. Organize into pairs those who are praying for healing. At each healing station have a small bowl of oil placed on a simple altar. You might want to also have a box of tissues available for each pair of healers.

Instructions. After everyone has gathered for the service, the leader introduces the service to the group and explains how the service will take place. Here is a sample introduction for this service:

Welcome to our evening healing service. I want to say a few words about this service to help you understand why we are holding it and how it will progress. We offer a service for healing because it is part of the practice of Jesus. Jesus is a healer and the Scriptures are filled with accounts of Jesus inviting people to bring their needs to him for healing. As Christians, followers of Jesus, we keep the same practice.

We don't know what happens in a healing service. We can't control or promise how the Holy Spirit will work. In James 5:16 we are told, "Pray for one another, so that you may be healed." That is why we are here. As Christians we are called to invite people to bring their needs to God and to pray for healing.

In the service tonight you may want to ask for heal-ing of a physical nature. Or you may want to ask for emotional or spiritual healing. You may want to ask for healing for a friend or family member or a situation in the world. These are also appropriate. You may want to use this time to mark a healing that has already taken place. That also is welcomed this evening.

Here is how this service will take place: Following the reading of Scripture there will be a few minutes of silence. We'll then have a song that will bring us out of silence. During this singing a group of us will come forward to set up healing stations. They will come to the table (or altar) at the front of the sanctuary and take a bowl of oil. They will then go in pairs to dif-ferent locations around the sanctuary. (At this point it's important to tell the group where these stations will be.)

After they have gone to their stations, they will spend some time praying for each other. When this is finished, they will face the group. As soon as they are facing the group, you are welcome to come forward. When you go to one of the stations say your name [if people are unfamiliar with one another] *and tell them your prayer request. They will pray with you and then offer to anoint your forehead with the sign of the cross.*

When you are not at one of the healing stations, we ask that you would lift this room in prayer. Spend this time praying for those who are coming forward so this room will be filled with God's healing presence.

Are there any questions?

This service format is as follows:

Quietly gather. The space should invite prayer and silent reflection as people quietly enter—candles, sacred images, and a lack of chatty conversation.

Singing. Once people have gathered, the song leader begins to sing. This singing is prayer, in the tradition of Christian chant. Songs are simple—often featuring one or two lines from Scripture that are sung continuously. Participants are encouraged to sing but also may enjoy just listening, allowing the music to wash over them.

Word. Read a passage in which someone received healing from Jesus. Read the passage twice, the second time a bit slower than the first. Allow a few minutes for silent prayer.

Song. This might be a recorded song or something led with the group. As the group sings, healers take oil from the altar, pair off, and go to different points around the room. It's important to have people spaced so their conversations will be private. Once at the station they pray for each another—this is the opportunity for the healers to receive prayers. Once a pair has finished praying, they turn and face the group in a posture of welcome.

Prayers of healing. Once the healers face the group, people are welcome to go to one of the healing stations for prayers. Participants come forward individually, with each person sharing his or her name and prayer concern. The healers then pray for that person. It is good for the healers to ask permission before making any physical contact. Usually one of the healers prays aloud over the person, and then the second healer anoints the person's forehead and gives some words of blessing—for example, "Know that you are a child of God." The healers may want to alternate roles for each person who comes forward. When it seems no one else is coming forward, the healers return the oil to the front table and resume their seats among the group.

The Lord's Prayer. At the close of spoken prayers, the leader invites the group to say the Lord's Prayer.

Singing. The song leader then leads the group in a final chant.

Quietly depart/Passing of peace/Eucharist. The leader offers a simple closing prayer. If there is time, I've found it can be quite moving to have Eucharist following the prayers of healing.

Prayer for Peace

God longs not only for the healing of individuals but also for the healing of the systems and structures— the principalities and powers that twist and obfuscate God's truth and love. Jesus was a peacemaker, and as lovers of Jesus we, too, seek to end violence, war, prejudice, environmental destruction, and all the ways in which human beings harm and demean one another.

For centuries Christians have turned to the Prayer of St. Francis as a source of guidance, encouragement, and conviction. The prayer reads:

Lord, make me an instrument of Thy peace;

Where there is hatred, let me sow love;

Where there is injury, pardon;

Where there is doubt, faith;

Where there is despair, hope;

Where there is darkness, light;

And where there is sadness, joy.

O Divine Master,

Grant that I may not so much seek to be consoled

as to console;

To be understood, as to understand;

To be loved, as to love;

For it is in giving that we receive;

It is in pardoning that we are pardoned;

And it is in dying that we are born to eternal life.

Amen.

I've found that this prayer carries the violence, prejudice, and envy within us to the surface for healing, while simultaneously drawing out the Holy Spirit's desire in us for peace and compassion. There are many ways to use this prayer, but here's one exercise that gives youth the time and space to allow this prayer to sink down into their bones:

Preparation. Prepare a place of prayer. Hand out copies of the Prayer of St. Francis along with a pencil or pen. Explain the steps of the prayer exercise.

Sending out. Invite young people to find a place in the room where they can pray undisturbed. I especially like to use this prayer when we're outdoors where students can take their time and find a place under the sky. Invite youth to become aware of God's presence, just resting in the God who creates life.

First reading. Gently read the Prayer of St. Francis, asking students to read along with you in silence. When you finish say, "Notice the words that stick with you as you finish hearing the prayer." Give them a minute or two of silence.

Second reading. Before reading the prayer a second time, invite the youth to pay attention to the people or situations that come to them as they hear it read. "Where do you encounter hatred, injury, doubt, despair? Maybe it's at school, in our town, or through the news. As you hear the words of St. Francis, write down the names and/or situations where God's peace is needed."

Third reading. Ask students to notice what feelings are being evoked as you read the prayer a third time. Have them set down their papers and place their hands over their hearts. Read the passage slowly, pausing at the end of each line so the words can sink in. Then ask, "What feelings do you notice within you?" Encourage them to circle any words that seem particularly evocative.

Final reading. Have students close their eyes. Ask them to listen for God's calling: "What is God's invitation to you as you read these words? How is God drawing you to respond?" After reading the prayer one last time slowly, invite students to journal prayerfully about the ways they sense God calling them to embody this prayer in the world.

Sending out. Ask kids to take a copy of the prayer home and place it in some prominent place—maybe on their dresser, their computer, in their locker, or some other prominent place. Ask them to try to pray this prayer each day, preferably as they begin their day, and see how it affects how they interact with others. When the group reconvenes, ask students about their experiences in praying the Prayer of St. Francis.

—∞∞∞—

About a month after the September 11, 2001, World Trade Center tragedy, I held a discussion on prayer with a group of high school students while their parents and pastors looked on. I asked the students how they were praying. Some of the youth confessed they were finding it difficult to pray, since they knew that many of the people in the twin towers had prayed for God to save them, yet God didn't respond. Others reflected on the fact that the men who flew the planes into the towers were praying for strength to complete their horrific mission—and those prayers, it seemed, were answered. One boy asked, "How can I pray when God ignores the innocent and allows these 'bad guys' to hurt people?"

This kind of sharing made many of the adults in the room anxious and upset. Although they were supposed to be silently observing our conversation, many of the adults interrupted the youth to defend God or condemn the terrorists. One pastor, upset that many of the youth expressed so much doubt and reluctance to pray because of the attack, stood up and told them in an admonishing tone that God had a reason for allowing the attack, and we could all be assured that the terrorists were in hell while the innocent who died were safe with God in heaven. If we wanted to join God in heaven, we should cease doubting and start praying again. The pastor spoke with an authority that negated all discussion. The youth looked down, no longer willing to share their real doubts and questions.

Then one brave, or maybe naive, 14-year-old spoke up. She said she had not had any break in her prayer life. She still prayed to God each night before bed, but recently God had given new images to her in prayer: "In my prayer I see all the people who have died—the terrorists, the passengers on the planes, and the people from the world trade towers. They're all sitting in a circle, and Jesus is there with them trying to help them talk about what happened and understand one another." She paused for a while and then added, "So I guess you could say I've been praying for all the people who were killed—the victims *and* the terrorists. Praying that Jesus is going to find a way to bring them together." I sat still, dumbstruck by this profound vision of grace and reconciliation.

Then another of the pastors slid his chair around the perimeter of the youth circle so he could face the girl who'd spoken: "I think we need a reality check here. I saw a cartoon the other day in which these terrorists were all sitting in hell. One guy leans over to the other and says, 'What happened to our heavenly heroes' welcome?' I think that's much closer to how God has dealt with those guys. Believe me, God is not caring for those murderers." The girl who had spoken became embarrassed and bent her head to the floor.

I don't know if the young girl's prayer was really from God or not. What I do know is that it sounded like Jesus—the Jesus who ate with Jews and tax collectors, with Roman soldiers and powerful religious leaders, with lepers, Samaritan women, prostitutes, and cripples. It sounded like the Jesus who prayed from the cross, asking God to forgive his killers, because they had no idea what they were doing.

An hour after talking with the young people, I gave a keynote talk on the nature of prayer in troubled times. Sitting in the front row were the youth who had been sharing their experiences of prayer following the September 11 attack. After talking about the various ways we're called to pray in the midst of suffering, I ended my talk by sharing the image of healing and reconciliation the 14-year-old girl had been praying.

When we invite youth to pray for healing, we're inviting them into the center of human sin and darkness. It's a fearful place—a place where human beings can get stuck, depressed, vengeful, self-protective, and hurtful. And yet it's where all prayer ends up, bringing light, grace, peace, and reconciliation to all that is outcast both within us and within the world.

Blessed be the healers,
blessed be the peacemakers,
blessed be the 14-year-old girls,
brave enough to see enemies sitting with one another
in the presence of Jesus.

19 Receive

He breathed on them and said to them, "Receive the Holy Spirit."

—JOHN 20:22

God is a gift. We may sometimes treat God like a burden, a demand, a sorrow, a disappointed parent, an unreachable dream, or an angry tyrant—but we are sorely confused. God is a gift—a gift as real and sweet as the plate of red strawberries my wife has just set next to me.

Much of the suffering in this life comes about because we don't know how to receive gifts. When my eldest son Noah was two years old, he had no understanding of a traditional North American Christmas. We decorated a tree, told him the story of Jesus' birth, and sang Christmas carols. On Christmas Eve we convinced Noah to set out cookies and carrots for a large, bearded man and his deer. Noah took all of this in without question. On Christmas morning we brought him out to see the tree overflowing with wrapped presents. We pointed to his red stocking now bulging with candy and toys, and asked him to marvel over the half-eaten cookies and carrots set on the hearth. "What do you think, Noah?" we asked, wanting to receive his joy and surprise. "Messy," was all he could say.

We set him down and placed his stocking on his lap. He looked inside and pulled out a tiny yellow car. He smiled at Mom then turned and smiled at Dad. A little car! How wonderful! If you watch our family video, you'll see Noah stand up and push that mechanical wonder over carpet and furniture while making little growling engine sounds. It's clear that our two-year-old would be quite happy to spend a good hour or two playing with his new car. But this isn't the way we do Christmas in the United States. The toy car was just a teaser, an appetizer, a dressing for the main course of gifts still wrapped and waiting.

If you were forced to sit through the whole 1997 Yaconelli Family Christmas video, you'd see an important, yet unfortunate, example of North American socialization. Noah, unaware that opening presents is a task to get through, receives each present with an unhurried wonder and delight. He examines each present slowly, carefully, often content to simply play with the ribbon and packaging without any need to see what the package contains. His parents, on the other hand, are anxious for him to speed up. You see us press Noah again and again to set his new toy aside and open another gift. You watch as Noah tries to take in each gift. You can feel his desire to examine, explore, and play with each present. But this is Christmas morning in California—there is no time to savor and receive; there are more gifts to open! So you see Noah begin to glaze over as he tries not to get drawn in by the pure pleasure of what's being given. You watch him begin to lose his ability to receive, until finally, thankfully, his parents see what's happening. The assembly line of gifts is brought to a halt. The unopened gifts are placed back under the tree. The opened presents are set back against a wall, and Noah is allowed to take his time and enjoy each little wonder, one at a time, lost in play and reverie. It took our two-year-old a month to open his Christmas gifts.

Whether it's the overstimulation, the culture of multitasking, the utilitarian work ethic to "make every second count," or simply the innumerable experiences of being given love that was fraught with guilt and obligations, we don't really know how to receive God and God's love. We don't really trust that God is a free gift. We focus on the conditions, the demands, the work, the sacrifice—not realizing that when we are unable to receive God's love and presence as a gift, we are unable to see that sacrifice, self-discipline, service, and suffering are not burdens, but simply the gratitude we offer, freely, gladly, in response to God's love.

Every time we invite youth to pray, we are like a good parent who sets a child down and places a treasure box on the child's lap. That present, however, is nothing like the material gifts we seek to accumulate that wear out, disintegrate, or become lost or stolen (Luke 12:33). The gift we seek to help young people receive is the gift of God, an "unfailing treasure." When we are able to receive God and God's way of life, we give God pleasure. "It is your Father's good pleasure to give you the kingdom," Jesus tells us (Luke 12:32). And so the real hope of all prayer is not only that we will give ourselves to God, but more importantly that we might allow Jesus to breathe on us and hear him say to us, "Receive the Holy Spirit." Receive the gift, receive the treasure, receive the miracle of God's love.

To receive God in prayer is a gift, one we can't force or control. In the Christian tradition the experience of receiving God in prayer is called contemplation. To read the experiences of contemplation within the lives of various praying Christians is to receive a kaleidoscope of images as rich, unique, and varied as people in the world. John of the Cross referred to it as "silent love." Teresa of Avila in the *Interior Castle* describes, "It's as if a tiny streamlet enters the sea from which it will find no way of separating itself, or as if in a room there were two large windows through which the light streamed in; it enters in different places but it all becomes one." Contemplation is an experience of being bathed in God's love and presence. It's an awareness of God, attained not through rational thought but through love. It is the experience Jesus refers to when he says, "Abide in me" (John 15:4), or what the psalmist speaks of when he writes, "Be still, and know" (Psalm 46:10) or describes a child resting on her mother's lap (Psalm 131:2). Contemplation in prayer is when the work of prayer ceases and we simply bathe in God's love in humility and gratitude.

Because it is a gift from God, prayerful contemplation can come over us at any time. Prayer only helps us become hospitable to this experience. All the prayers described in this book, with their emphases on rest and receptivity, help expand the capacity of young people to receive and welcome God's love. The exercises listed below, however, are even more intentional in focusing the hearts of young people on welcoming and receiving God's love and peace.

Prayer of the Heart

When my friend Kirk was a teenager, he often prayed while lying on his back, hands over his heart. There was something about feeling his heartbeat as he prayed that helped him slow down and center himself in God.

At the close of a youth group meeting, before sending kids off to bed during a camp or retreat, or anytime it feels like I need to help the youth slow down and open themselves to God, I'll ask students to lie on their backs, close their eyes, and place both hands over their hearts. I'll then let them spend a few moments just noticing their heartbeats, the place where Jesus is knocking, seeking to enter into their lives. Sometimes I read a verse or two about Jesus knocking on our hearts, or God's Spirit dwelling within us. In silence I invite the youth to listen to their hearts in the quiet, as if those heartbeats are a prayer to God. If there are words of prayer that come to them, I invite them to speak them to God, and then return to their heartbeat—the rhythm of their own lives, lived in the presence of God.

Other lines from Scripture that can be fruitful for this form of prayer include "Be still, and know that I am God!" (Psalm 46:10) or "Into your hands I commend my spirit" (Luke 23:46).

The Jesus Prayer

A more ancient form of contemplative prayer is called "The Jesus Prayer."[49] The early desert fathers and mothers fled to the desert to make themselves available to God in prayer and solitude. Eventually they began to pray the prayer of the two blind men crying out to Jesus, "Kyrie Eleison" or "Lord, have mercy" (Matthew 20:31). These early spiritual seekers would pray these words in rhythm with their breathing, seeking to move the words of this prayer into the very rhythms of their heart until they found themselves praying "without ceasing." Believers in the Orthodox tradition continue to pray the Jesus Prayer throughout the day. Although it's been modified into various forms over the centuries, the most common wording is "Jesus Christ, Son of God, have mercy on me." As the Jesus Prayer is repeated over and over it moves from a prayer of the mouth to a prayer of the heart.

Downtime: Helping Teenagers Pray

---

[49] For a description of one person's attempt to pray this prayer read the spiritual classic, Helen Bacovcin, translator. *The Way of a Pilgrim and the Pilgrim Continues His Way.* (Image Doubleday, 1985). For more on the Jesus Prayer read Lev Gillet, *The Jesus Prayer,* (St. Vladimir's Seminary, 1987).

When leading this prayer with young people it's important to first give some of the context of the prayer. You might read Mark 10:46-52, and talk about the blindness of Bartimaeus, as well as his desire and persistence to be healed. Take some time to allow kids to reflect on their own blindness to the life of God as well as their own need for healing. You might have students reflect on the ways in which they, like Bartimaeus, are surrounded by voices both around and within them that seek to quiet and stifle their prayer.

After this discussion, explain the steps of the Jesus Prayer. Let kids know the hope of this prayer is that, as the words are repeated over and over within us, they might draw out our own desire for healing and begin to draw our heart's attention to the presence and mercy of Jesus.

Begin with an opening prayer asking the Holy Spirit to help the students focus their minds and hearts on the presence of Jesus. Then invite everyone to begin repeating the words of the Jesus Prayer. You can have students do this out loud, in gentle whispers. I've found it best to let students walk outside or find a place alone within a church to recite the words. This is how the prayer was done in its earliest forms. By reciting the words of the prayer out loud, the mouth, ears, and mind are all engaged in the prayer. If this seems awkward or impractical, have students repeat the words of the prayer within themselves. If kids are given the freedom to walk and move about, I'd give them a half hour to pray; less time if space is limited.

Let students know that as they repeat the words prayerfully they may notice an invitation to move more deeply into prayer. They may notice the words becoming their own, expressing the real desires within their hearts.

Be sure to talk about the many distractions students will experience as they pray: Interior thoughts and memories, outside noises, etc. Just as in other forms of prayer, remind students that, when they notice they're distracted, they should simply return to the words of the prayer.

The early desert mothers and fathers believed that over time, as a person engaged the Jesus Prayer, the prayer would create an abiding sense of God's presence. As we repeat the words "Jesus, have mercy" over time, we may have a growing sense the prayer is no longer something we do, but instead has become who we are. At moments like this, the work of prayer ceases, and we find ourselves open and available to the Spirit. Let students know that such experiences of abiding in the Spirit are gifts—gifts the Jesus Prayer helps us receive.

Centering Prayer

Although the term *centering prayer* and its particular format came into being only within the past 40 years, the prayer is a summary of various forms of silent, contemplative practices that date back to the very beginnings of Christianity.[50] This form of prayer trusts the direct and immediate availability of God, the "indwelling Christ," who is nearer than one's own heartbeat.

Centering prayer is a simplified form of contemplative prayer and finds its roots in the final stages of *lectio divina* (see chapter 8).[51] Although we may think of prayer as thoughts or feelings about God expressed in words, this is only one expression of prayer. In contemplative prayer we seek the full opening of mind and heart, soul and body—our whole being—to the Spirit of God, the ultimate mystery, utterly beyond thoughts, words, images, and emotions. We open our awareness to the God who dwells within us—closer than breathing, closer than thinking, closer than choosing, closer than consciousness itself.

---

[50] Forms of centering or silent prayer can be found in the writings of the early desert fathers and mothers, Julian of Norwich, John of the Cross, and other mystical theologians, and are most clearly articulated in the anonymously written fourteenth-century devotional, *The Cloud of Unknowing*. One of the modern "founders" of centering prayer, M. Basil Pennington, sees centering prayer as a direct outgrowth of *lectio divina*. For more on the history and tradition of centering prayer see "The Christian Contemplative Tradition and Centering Prayer," *Centering Prayer in Daily Life and Ministry*, Thomas Keating and Gustav Reininger, ed.(Continuum, 1998)

[51] Basil Pennington describes this history in his book *Centering Prayer* (Image, 1982).

Within the silence of centering prayer, we consent to the power of God's presence and unconditional love working within us. Here is a modified version of centering prayer based on the method devised by Thomas Keating.[52]

Have students sit comfortably in a prayerful space. Light a candle as a reminder of God's presence, and then describe the method of centering prayer. Explain that each student is to choose a sacred word with which to pray. This word will be a symbol of their intention to be with God, an expression of their desire to be in God's loving presence. Examples include *Jesus, Lord, Abba, Love, Mercy, Stillness, Faith, Trust, Shalom,* and *Amen.* Once everyone has selected a word, remind them to stick with the word—don't get caught up worrying if some other word might be more "spiritual" and produce "better" results. Tell students that the word is simply a reminder of their desire to be with God. What's significant in this prayer is their intention (to be with God), not their particular word.

Before you begin to pray, tell students how long the silence will last. (I recommend about 10 minutes.) It's important to emphasize that it's common during silent prayer for our minds to wander into different thoughts, memories, and fantasies. We may

[52] The method of centering prayer is found in many of Keating's writings including *Open Mind, Open Heart* and *Centering Prayer in Daily Life and Ministry.*

even forget we're praying. Make sure you tell kids that these experiences are not unusual. It's similar to when we try to listen to a good friend—sometimes our minds wander, we think of other things, we think of words we want to say, or we get distracted and forget to listen. It's the same in centering prayer; we try to direct our heart's attention to God, but often we find ourselves distracted. When students feel distracted, they should simply go back to the prayer word as a way of bringing attention back to God.

After responding to any questions students might have, invite them to close their eyes and settle themselves for prayer. Encourage them to pray in a spirit of warm hospitality—as if they were waiting to welcome a close friend or family member. Then invite them to begin briefly and silently introducing their sacred word as the symbol of their consent to God's presence and action within and around them. Thomas Keating suggests introducing the sacred word "inwardly and as gently as laying a feather on a piece of cotton." As they pray, it can be helpful to remind them to gently return to their sacred word if they feel distracted. Sometimes, after a minute of silence I'll say, "Notice how far your mind has wandered in prayer? Now say your word gently as a way of bringing yourself back to God's love."

At the end of the prayer period, invite students to remain silent for a few moments with their eyes closed. Then lead the group in the Lord's Prayer or some other formal prayer as a way of drawing the prayer to a close.

Make sure you give students a chance to share their experiences of the prayer. It's important, again, to remind students that everyone experiences distractions in prayer; otherwise they may judge themselves spiritually inadequate. It's also important to remember that the fruit of this prayer is in how we live our daily lives, not always in the prayer itself.

—◯◯◯—

The anonymous author of *The Cloud of Unknowing* once wrote, "God is the best friend you've ever had." In the presence of a close friend, we can be ourselves. There is no need for posturing or pretending. It is the same with God. By making space for kids to spend time with God, we help them recognize they are not alone in this world. We invite them to see that, beneath the hustle of modern life, there is real compassion, real inspiration, real truth, and real love just waiting to be noticed. Adolescents straining to gain a sense of identity will not only discover God's companionship, but just as important, they'll discover that they too have the capacity for great love and friendship. They too have the capacity to bring food to the hungry, sight to the blind, comfort to the mourning, peace and justice to the oppressed. As Jesus said to his friends not long before he left this life, "the one who believes in me will also do the works that I do and, in fact, will do greater works than these..." (John 14:12).

20 Sweet as Honey

Mortal, eat this scroll that I give you and fill
your stomach with it. Then I ate it; and in my
mouth it was as sweet as honey.
—EZEKIEL 3:3

When I was five years old, my grandfather, Monroe Free-
man, hitched his round, silver dollar trailer to his truck and
drove me up to the San Bernardino Mountains. It was spring-
time, the clover was blooming, and my grandfather, a weekend beekeeper, needed to collect honey. In silence we drove
from freeway to rural highway to mountain lane to dirt road
until finally my grandfather, whom I affectionately called
"Popo," rambled the truck off into a mountainside meadow.
He parked the truck in a field of clover, and instructed me
to stay inside, out of the bright sun. Then he walked a few

hundred yards to a stack of white wooden boxes that looked like an abandoned wedding cake sitting among the clover.

I sat on the musty, quilted bed and felt the warm Southern California wind gently swirling the sweet smell of clover blossoms in and through the trailer doors. A few times I sat up and looked out across the meadow to watch my grandfather. Dressed in a white cloak and veiled hat, he moved slowly and deliberately among the tiny black bees, swinging a small smoking canister like an Easter priest processing incense through the congregation.

Restless, I jumped up and down on the springless bed, then sat on the steps of the trailer, then returned to jumping. Seduced by the sun and green hillside, and against my grandfather's instructions, I stepped out of the trailer. Without any particular destination I tromped through the waist-high clover, running my hands over the tiny blossoms. At some point, I felt a tiny vibration tickle my hand. Startled, I stopped and noticed a cluster of round flowers attended by a brotherhood of gold-and-black-coated bees. It was fascinating to watch their dark, thorny legs high-step through the soft, mustard carpet of each flower. Wanting a closer look, I knelt down to bring my eyes level with the working bees. I don't know how long I stayed kneeling among the clover; I do know the moment felt eternal—the warm summer wind, the gently swaying field, the bees delicately moving from blossom to blossom. I knelt in timeless wonder while a warm contentment moved through my body, like being embraced from the inside out.

My grandfather came up behind me hauling a five-gallon bucket heavy with honeycombs. "Are you praying?" he asked playfully. I stood quickly, worried I was in trouble for leaving the trailer. Popo's hat was unveiled and cocked back on his head. Smiling, he reached down. "Here. Try this." He handed me a small melting glob of honey. I placed it in my mouth. It was warm, surprisingly thick, and stung my whole mouth sweet. "It's wax in the middle, so don't swallow it."

I chewed carefully, sucking out the little pores of liquid flowers, until I had a chewing gum wad of wax. "What were you doing out here?" my grandfather asked, setting the bucket beside me. I looked at him tentatively, still wondering if he was upset. "Looking at bees," I said. He nodded his head, reached down to hand me another soft shard of honeycomb, and said gently, "Well, it seemed like you were praying."

All throughout my growing up I would reflect on this moment among the bees and clover. I had felt the edge of something, something mysterious and wonderful, some secret wholeness, something beyond the reach of my own mind, something holy and eternal, some kind of beauty at the center of the shimmering world. It's only now—now that I'm 40 years old, now that my grandfather has passed away, now that the clover field has been leveled and turned into a housing development, now that 70 percent of the wild honeybees have disappeared from North America—that I can finally give a reply to my grandfather's question.

"Yes, you were right. I was praying."

Young people today are increasingly diseased by society's command to consume, accumulate, and succeed. In a society sickened by greed, prayer becomes a necessary medicine, a healing balm. For young people today, prayer is downtime. It is a break from a culture that has lost its mind—a culture whose addiction to speed is killing the earth's very ability to sustain life.

When we pray, we enter into the life of God. Prayer requires a certain kind of withdrawal from the busyness of our lives. It is prayer that gives us perspective, reminding us that life does not have to be driven by our own carnal desires. It is prayer that expands the heart, increasing our capacity for joy, friendship, beauty, compassion, generosity, and love. It is prayer that empowers us to live out our gifts, release our addictions, and tend the suffering places within and around us. It is prayer that inspires us for acts of justice and mercy and emboldens us toward radical acts of friendship and peace.

We minister among people who enjoy the greatest accumulation of material wealth in the history of humankind, and yet often carry the most emaciated and anemic of souls. As Mother Teresa once said, "You in the West have the spiritually poorest of the poor...it is easy to give a plate of rice to a hungry person, to furnish a bed to a person who has no bed, but to console or to remove the bitterness, anger, and loneliness that comes from being spiritually deprived, that takes a long time."[53]

The most difficult aspect of our ministries among the spiritually poor is that the problem is so easily hidden. Has there ever been another society that has produced so many spiritual books, workshops, retreat centers, worship experiences, churches, and sacred fashion accessories? The culture in which we minister seems ignorant to the fact that the plethora

[53] Becky Benenate & Joseph Durepos, ed., *No Greater Love*, (MJF Books, 1997).

of Christian experiences, consumer products, and activities only belies our spiritual deprivation and disconnection from God. Why do we create so many clanging Christian gongs when "God alone" is all that's needed?

As youth ministers we seek to help young people develop strong and healthy souls. We seek to tend lives that are rooted in the rich soil of God's love. We seek to cultivate within young people enough trust and faith in God that they might resist the powers and principalities that diminish them. As companions of Jesus, much of our work is a simple effort to awaken young people to the riches of God that wait within and around them. "Only through prayer do we come to know our own goodness and the love that God has for us," Brother Rogers counsels. Through prayer we seek to help young people become aware, receptive, and responsive to this love in the midst of all things, all people, and all experiences. We "hope" young people into companionship with Jesus so they might learn how to live as free and whole human beings.

—⟨∾⟩—

Twenty-eight years after collecting honey with my grandfather, I found myself deeply discouraged and exhausted. I had spent five years trying to hold three jobs simultaneously—volunteer youth minister, full-time director of the Youth Ministry and Spirituality Project, and adjunct teacher at San Francisco Theological Seminary. On top of this, I had two young children who were full of life and energy and seemed to have little need for sleep. Exhausted and disheartened by my propensity to overschedule myself, I took two days to pray and fast in the Mendocino Mountains. I camped atop a dry hillside scattered with brown-paper-leafed oak trees. This was July, and the days were hot and dusty. The only life I saw was a rattlesnake that moved slowly through my campsite unperturbed by my attempts to clap and stomp it away.

On the second day of fasting, I found I was becoming more and more aware of the harried and hyperactive drivenness of my life. This awareness was particularly painful and humiliating since most of my work life was about teaching youth workers and students to spend more time in prayer and Sabbath rest. Hot, hungry, and disheartened, I hiked down to a nearby creek. The creek bed was so cool and shaded that I immediately knelt down in the water. After enjoying the relief from the heat, and without any intention on my part, I suddenly discovered myself pleading for God's mercy: "Lord, have mercy. Help me to live," I prayed over and over. I was broken, in need of God's guidance and grace.

After a while my prayer ceased, and I sat back on my heels, the creek water passing over my legs. I looked, unhurriedly, down the tree-lined stream and noticed a small black flicker making its way above the water. I followed the flying speck until I could see it was some sort of bee, buzzing zigzag toward me, right at eye level. Unafraid and slowed from fasting, I sat watching the winged insect until suddenly, surprisingly, it buzzed right up to my face, brushed my lips, and then turned and flew back up the creek bed. I sat delighted by this small kiss, then watched as a second, then a third, then a fourth humming honeybee came weaving down the crooked creek to touch my lips, then return toward the water's source.

Then memory struck. I remembered the long leisurely afternoon in my grandfather's clover field. I remembered the sense of leisure and delight I used to experience as a child. I remembered kneeling in the blossoms at five years old, full of wonder and awe at the newfound world. I realized how much I missed and needed time with God. I sat weeping repentantly while bees kissed my lips until it seemed to me that I could taste the sweet nectar of flowers at the edge of my mouth.

It is said that the ancient teachers of the Torah on the first day of class would place a dollop of honey on their students' tongues and then let them savor the taste so a student's first association with the Holy Scripture was sweet pleasure. It is this sweetness of God that this book has sought to recall and inspire.

The truth is we can't give young people happiness. We can't take away their pain and suffering; we can't shield them from the temptations that play upon their weaknesses and yearnings 24 hours a day. In the midst of a suffering world, it sometimes feels like we have so little to offer young people—some fleeting friendships, a few nights of fun and understanding...Our real gift is to give them God—a God who will be sweet and nourishing food for them. What we can offer even the most troubled teenager is prayer. We can teach young people that, in the midst of pain, confusion, and brokenness, they can turn toward love. They can stop and fall down among the clover, among the blossoms, among the words and promises of Scripture and hear the One who whispers to each of us, "Taste and see that the Lord is good."

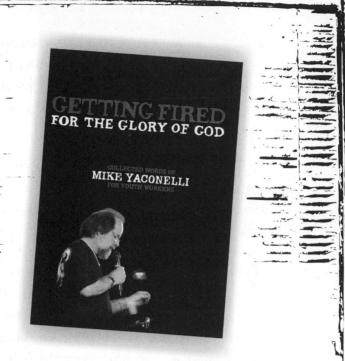

Years after his death, Christians across the world turn to the words of Mike Yaconelli to uncover the divine mischief, the shameless truth-telling, the love of kids, and the passion for Jesus that make youth ministry an irresistible calling.

Getting Fired for the Glory of God
Mike Yaconelli
RETAIL $16.99
ISBN 978-0-310-28358-4

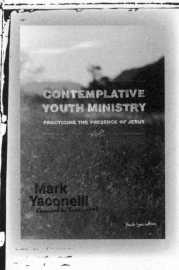